Foresight Infused Strategy Development

A How-To Guide for Using Foresight in Practice

Maree Conway

Published by Thinking Futures
Melbourne, Australia
Website: http://thinkingfutures.net

First published in ebook format 2016
This paperback version published 2019

Book Layout © 2014 BookDesignTemplates.com

ISBN: 9781095942482

CONTENTS

Acknowledgements

My approach to foresight is informed by my work in the then Foresight and Planning Unit at Swinburne University of Technology from 1999-2005, where I collaborated with Dr Joseph Voros (now in the Faculty of Business and Law at Swinburne), and Marcus Barber (now running Looking Up, Feeling Good). Apart from being wonderful collaborators, my conversations with Joe and doing workshops with Marcus taught me much about foresight, both conceptually and practically. Meeting Richard Slaughter (Foresight International) when he set up and ran the foresight program at Swinburne was fortuitous and gave me access to one of the leading minds of the foresight field.

My formal study in the Master's in Strategic Foresight course at Swinburne University gave me the intellectual grounding so essential for good and useful foresight work, and introduced me to Integral Futures which now forms the baseline for my work with people in organisations.

Joining the Association of Professional Futurists was a good move, exposing me to much of the leading thinking in the foresight domain and connecting me with people who were willing to share their knowledge and help others just starting out in the field. I have made good friends and learned much from these generous people and I thank them for that.

I've also drawn upon and adapted the work of many colleagues, whom I've cited in the book. I thank you here collectively for sharing your work so freely and allowing me to learn from your experience and practice. I also acknowledge the people I've worked with across the years – the learning both good and not so good that comes from every interaction with them has increased my capacity to use foresight well.

I have to thank here too all the people who have given me feedback since the ebook was published in 2016 about the content, how it has helped them in their work, and its value for them as a reference guide. I've left the content alone in this paper version as a result except for a few grammatical corrections.

Maree Conway
March 2016
April 2019

Preface

This book is designed to provide you with enough information to help you move away from conventional strategic planning and infuse foresight into your strategy development process. Like all publications from Thinking Futures, the book's purpose is to help people like you move beyond formulaic planning and superficial approaches to using foresight to craft futures ready strategy.

I learned about using foresight at Swinburne University. When I decided to leave Swinburne in 2004, I spent some time reviewing my career to work out exactly what it was that I wanted to do. I was looking for my career purpose which by then I knew must include foresight. After about three months of reflection and interrogating myself with every career assessment tool I could find, this is what I wrote early one Sunday morning while sitting at the kitchen table:

> *I want to contribute to increasing the understanding of the value of foresight approaches in organisations by working with individuals, with a focus on recognising our collective responsibility for future generations.*

My belief in our collective responsibility for future generations is why I do what I do, and I write more about that in Chapter 2. When I established Thinking Futures as my foresight practice in 2007 however, I fell into the trap of using what I now see as the conventional consulting approach. The consultant, facilitator, expert approach, accepting whatever work that came my way. I was so excited to be working full time in the foresight field that I forgot about my purpose, my need to work with individuals.

Over the past couple of years, I've returned to that statement I wrote in 2004 and reframed what I do: I work with individuals in organisations who are serious about using foresight, who want to deepen their understanding of change and who are ready to transform their strategy development to be futures ready. I want our organisations to use foresight to morph into social and business entities that face the future. More than that, my hope is that organisations will work together to ensure that they are not only futures ready but also to ensure that we have futures ready individuals, societies and a planet that is sustainable in the long term.

I can't do that alone. Human agency is at the core of this shift to futures ready - people who work together to understand change that matters for their organisation, who create preferred futures and who work collaboratively to move towards that future. To make that shift happen requires us to redesign strategy processes and open up how we think about and anticipate the future.

Right now, too many consultants are paid to come into organisations and use their favourite strategic planning model or push their software. Facilitators are paid to come in to run planning workshops and organisations pay a lot of money for access to generic, off the shelf reports on the future of anything you like, or commission their own reports. None of those things are necessarily a bad thing but on their own, they do little to generate long term change to make an organisation futures ready - because the strategic thinking of people in the organisation has been outsourced.

If what I just described sounds familiar, you are letting someone else doing your strategic thinking for you. Their view of what matters for your organisation is being used as the starting point for strategy development.

Any future view you develop from someone else's starting point in not owned by you, not felt by you. You might have used experts (and they know best don't they?), their process might be quicker (and you are busy aren't you?) and you will get a strategic plan (and you have to tick that box don't you?). You will also get strategy that fails when it meets the future, because strategy without your people at its core is strategy without a future. That's not what I do.

I start with individuals. The person who knows they have a foresight capacity and wants to use it in their organisation. The person who knows their thinking has to shift and how their organisation deals with change has to shift. The person who knows instinctively there has to be a better way. There is, and that's why I wrote this book. It's about how you can use foresight in practice to build your ability to face the future and to help build an organisational foresight capacity. We need foresight if we are to understand in a systemic way the breadth and depth of change all around us **and** develop proactive responses to that change today.

You will find many books on trends shaping the future, about what the future might look like in 'x' number of years, how the foresight field is emerging and the latest methods to use. If that's what you are looking for, this is not the book for you. This is the book I wish I'd had when I was asked to 'do foresight' at Swinburne University in 1999. It's a personal book, a sharing of my learning, knowledge and experience to give you the basics, so that you don't have to spend six months finding out about foresight like I did then. It's also a book focused on you, the individual, the person who wants to find out more about foresight and how to use it in your organisation.

The book is deliberately not written in a formal or scholarly style, although there are references throughout the text and I've included a selected reference list at the end of the book. I've included web links in the text wherever I can so you can access the material quickly. I've aimed the book at the beginner but experienced foresighters may find value in some places. As a practitioner, it's important that the content of this book is grounded in reality and that it does help you and others in your organisation understand both the value of using foresight and how to use it in practical ways in your strategy development. Let me know if I've achieved this aim.

Finally, what I write here is based on my experience using foresight with people in organisations since 1999. It reflects my focus on strategy development, the methods I use, the industries in which I have worked and the people with whom I have collaborated. I hope you find it useful. And, do get in touch when you are ready to use foresight in your organisation. You will know when it's time.

Terminology

Like any field, foresight has its own jargon. There are levels of depth in foresight work and the jargon can become more esoteric as you increase your depth of knowledge, focus and practice. The terms here are the ones I use most often.

Foresight is thinking about the future to inform decision making today. We use our foresight capacities every day. It is a cognitive capacity that we need to develop as individuals, as organisations and as a society. For individuals, it's usually an unconscious capacity and needs to be surfaced to be used in any meaningful way to inform decision making. For me though, foresight is different to the term futures.

Futures refers to the broad academic and professional field now developing globally as well as research, methods and tools that are available to us. The term 'futures' should be viewed as a collective noun, in the same way that we talk of 'economics' or 'politics'. The term is always plural because there is **always** more than one future available to us.

Foresight Infused Strategy is strategy developed using foresight approaches. People and collaboration are at the core of these approaches. It produces strategy that links what we know about the past and the present with the unknowns of the future to create stronger, futures ready strategy today.

Futures Ready Strategy is flexible strategy that positions your organisation to respond quickly and effectively to future challenges and uncertainties. It is strategy built on long term strategic thinking. Futures ready strategy allows proactive responses to change to be developed and implemented today or at a time in the future when a response becomes appropriate.

Foresight Readiness: the degree to which your organisation is ready to use foresight. I see three degrees of readiness that can be discerned in an organisation's culture: open to foresight, thinking about it but not yet convinced and closed to the idea.

Foresight Practitioners: I prefer this term because my experience has shown me that **futurists** unfortunately comes with connotations of prediction and crystal balls, as unfair and unreasonable as that may be. In addition, anyone can call themselves a futurist – it's a common term appropriated by anyone who wants to use it, as opposed to academically trained and professional futurists. For me, you need your foresight switch turned on to be able to claim to be a futurist and that only happens after you have been immersed in foresight concepts, principles and thinking.

Futurists: those who do foresight work as academics, consultants and practitioners within organisations.

Futures/Foresight Approaches: the tools, methods and thinking styles used to build an organisational foresight capacity, usually interdisciplinary, inclusive and participatory and not restricted to a particular philosophy, discipline or method.

Strategic Foresight: an organisational foresight capacity that informs the development of strategy, the development of which happens when there is a critical mass of foresight aware individuals in organisations.

Scenario Planning/Thinking: scenario planning is a familiar business method and it's often used as part of a broader foresight project. I prefer to call this process **scenario thinking** to highlight the importance of thinking in new ways about possible futures during scenario development. For me successful scenario projects only succeed if the scenario narratives are engaging and compelling, identify new strategic options **and** people report that their thinking about change and the future has shifted.

I also use the term **conventional** quite a bit in the book when referring to strategic planning. I use it in the sense of what we collectively understand strategic planning to be and how we use it to develop strategy using what are considered to be accepted and unquestioned standards and processes.

1 Introduction

Using foresight approaches in your strategy development will be one of the most challenging and intellectually stimulating things you might do in your career. Because you are reading this book, you are probably interested in finding out more about foresight and about how to:

- build a deeper understanding of change shaping your organisation's future,
- enhance the strategic thinking capability of people in your organisation,
- strengthen your organisational strategy development by integrating foresight approaches into your processes, and/or
- prepare your organisation to be able to respond more effectively and more proactively to its emerging future.

The book will move through the major phases of using foresight in strategy development. I mention the need to change the way you think about the future often because using foresight involves not only doing strategy differently but also thinking in new ways. It takes internal change in our minds and external change in our strategy development to use foresight successfully. By the end of the book, you should have enough information to determine both how to surface and use your foresight capacity and how to introduce foresight to your organisation.

Why Foresight and Foresight Infused Strategy?

It's a truism that organisations today exist in environments that are changing rapidly and increasing in complexity. Conventional methods of interpreting and understanding those environments work well when the world is comparatively stable. In such environments an organisation does not necessarily need a collaborative and organisation wide scanning, strategic thinking and planning capacity, since possible futures can be extrapolated with relative certainty and strategic choices are often quite clear.

We have not had those sorts of environments since the middle of the twentieth century. The environments in which organisations now exist are moving so quickly that future outcomes can no longer be assumed. Because our worlds are mired in complexity, there are often no obvious choices. A different approach to strategy development is needed.

Infusing your strategy development processes with foresight will allow you to strengthen the strategic thinking that ultimately informs your strategic plan, and ensure your strategy is futures ready – this is flexible strategy, ready for whatever challenges and opportunities the future brings to your doorstep.

It will not be easy. Because there are no facts about the future, you will need to convince people who are familiar and comfortable with quantitative data and evidence-based decision making that using images, imaginations and working with the inherent uncertainty of the future are valuable and essential additions to strategy development. You will come up against deeply held and often unquestioned assumptions about the way strategy **should** be developed, how your organisation **should** view the world in which it operates and how its future **will** evolve over time.

Conventional strategy models tend to centre on processes run by planners to develop and implement plans for the here and now, for action to be taken today. These processes will include words about the future that are usually written following some ad hoc mainstream trend analysis rather than an exploration by the whole organisation of what **might** happen to shape its future. The result is a single, business as usual future described in a plan upon which the organisation 'bets the farm'.

Such a plan built around business as usual is called the official scenario. When the official scenario fails because of unforeseen change in the external environment, an organisation tends to enter crisis mode and becomes reactive. Using foresight is one way of avoiding crisis management because it allows you to take the time to **think** more systemically about the future and to plan ahead of time to identify responses to those possible shifts in the external environment. By taking time to think, an organisation is anticipating the future rather than reacting to it and will be better prepared to adapt to change. Table 1 shows a set of questions asked when you are either reacting to change or anticipating the future. Both end with the same question but the starting point is quite different.

Table 1: Proactive and Reactive Strategy Questions

Reactive Strategy: Reacting to Change	Proactive Strategy: Anticipating the Future
What has happened?	What is happening?
What caused it to happen?	What is driving the change that will influence our future? What might our alternative futures be?
How do we respond now?	How might we respond today? What could be the long-term consequences of our actions today?
What will we do?	What will we do?

How to think about the future systemically is the least understood element of conventional strategy development, even though everyone would agree that strategy is developed to allow organisations to survive and be sustainable into the future. This book aims to give you the fundamentals, the how to of using foresight in your strategy development to help you anticipate rather than react to the future, to help your strategy become futures ready.

The Value of Foresight Approaches

Just how are foresight approaches different from conventional planning? Where's the value? This section provides my rationale for using foresight.

Using foresight allows us to take a forward view to identify possible, plausible and probable futures and then to develop a preferred future (see Chapter 3 for more information on different types of futures). A preferred future provides a long-term strategic focus that informs decision making today. Instead of giving in to the view that change is happening so quickly there's no point planning for the future, we instead use the future as the strategic end-point, something that helps us move ahead with clarity of purpose and that provides the ability and flexibility to mitigate challenges and grasp useful opportunities as they emerge.

Foresight approaches consider a wider range of issues and change across industries, including emerging issues and more general societal issues and trends. They also take a big picture, systems approach to identifying and understanding global change and look for systemic drivers of that change. Industries are shaped by this global change and not exploring it means you have an incomplete picture of change shaping your organisation's future. Trends are also not confined to particular industries and interactions, collisions and intersections between trends and across industries are explored in depth to identify potential strategic implications for your organisation.

Foresight work identifies and uses wider sources of information from both the mainstream and the periphery, as well as seeking to source tacit views, beliefs and ideas about the future held by individuals. This exposes people in organisations to different types of content about the future and helps to challenge individual and collective taken for granted ideas about what the future will be like.

Foresight approaches use a long-term time frame. Thinking systematically about the future is not about trying to get the future right through prediction, but rather ensuring you don't get it wrong. Potential longer-term impacts of decisions may not be visible if the time frame used in strategy is too short term. A longer-term time frame creates a strong context for your decision making today.

Foresight work aims to surface and challenge assumptions that underpin current thinking and decision making. These assumptions are often grounded in deeply held beliefs that are difficult to shift, even in the face of disconfirming evidence. Surfacing assumptions can therefore be hard work and asking individuals to recognise their blindspots and cognitive biases will usually be an uncomfortable experience. Trying to avoid this discomfort by dismissing the new and the different will only allow people to ignore the change that could disrupt their business models and make them irrelevant.

Foresight approaches allow strategy development to be an inclusive process. Because foresight is an innate human capacity, everyone in an organisation is capable of thinking strategically if given the opportunity and the information. Using foresight can allow staff to be involved in authentic ways in the process of creating a shared view of their organisation's future. Since staff will be asked to implement the strategy, enabling them to both shape and see themselves in the future embodied in that strategy is common sense.

Using foresight will help you see the big picture. The world is changing across all domains – social, political, technological, economic, environmental – and that change **is** connected globally and across industries. Crafting strategy without developing a deep and systemic understanding of this change and identifying what really matters for your organisation will make your strategy superficial and open to being irrelevant as soon as your plan is written.

Foresight work provides an opportunity to recognise that sometimes the opinions we hold so dear today may not be viewed as relevant or reasonable in the future. Here are some quotes that demonstrate the folly of letting your unquestioned assumptions get in the way of recognising the implications of change coming over the horizon.

- Inventions have long since reached their limit, and I see no hope for future development. *Roman engineer Sextus Julius Frontinus, 1st century AD*
- Louis Pasteur's theory of germs is ridiculous fiction. *Pierre Pachet, Professor of Physiology, Toulouse, 1872*
- Heavier than air flying machines are not possible. *Lord Kelvin, President of the Royal Society, 1895*
- The aeroplane will never fly. *Lord Haldane, British Minister of War, 1907*
- Stocks have reached what looks like a permanently high plateau. *Irving Fisher, Professor of Economics, Yale University, 1929*
- I think there is a world market for maybe 5 computers. *Thomas Watson, Chairman of IBM, 1943*
- Space flight is hokum. *Astronomer Royal, 1956*

- We don't like their sound, and guitar music is on the way out. *Decca Recording Co, rejecting the Beatles, 1962*
- But, what is it good for? *Attributed to an engineer at advanced systems division at IBM, commenting on the first microchip, 1968*
- There is no reason anyone would want a computer in their home. *Ken Olson, founder of Digital Equipment, 1977*
- 640k [of ram] ought to be enough for anybody. *Bill Gates, 1981*

These statements were probably considered to be realistic and accurate in the context of knowledge available at the time. They were made by experts so had an aura of credibility. It is only hindsight coupled with our knowledge of the present that allows us to recognise how short sighted these statements were. Yet, every time someone 'predicts' what's coming they are at risk of making a statement equally as silly as these. What is even worse is many of us accept these predictions are valid. They rarely are.

The future is characterised by uncertainty, complexity and much that we simply cannot yet know. More significantly, we do not know what we do not know. For anyone to claim absolute certainty about the future is at best well-intentioned but misguided and at worst, incredibly arrogant. Foresight has value because it allows us to acknowledge uncertainty and seek to better understand it, not try to explain it away with predictions.

Done well, using foresight moves thinking beyond the status quo and helps organisations prepare to respond to change proactively. We all know that being trapped in the status quo is a formula for crisis management when change arrives unannounced on your organisation's doorstep. If you use foresight and scan at the edge, at the periphery where the seeds of the future are emerging, you can gain competitive advantage. You will expand your thinking about what is possible in the future so you can develop products and services that will matter in that future. You will be futures ready.

Moving Beyond Case Studies and Best Practice

Context matters when using foresight. If you have relied on case studies or best practice to use foresight or copied an approach used in another organisation, then you may have a problem. Certainly there are a set of tools like scenario thinking that are available to everyone, but how they are tailored and applied must be unique for each organisation.

When I am talking with people about using foresight in practice people often ask for case studies or best practice examples. I usually resist and they resist right back. Why do I resist? Much good foresight work is not public but rather considered proprietary although an article by Farrington, Henson, & Crews (2012) is an example of what is shared. It's difficult to respond to requests for case studies and best practice with much detail therefore so I usually share my experience of using foresight or provide a list of companies that I think use it well. But I resist mainly because I am dubious about the value that emerges from our apparent preoccupation with best practice and case studies.

Best Practice

It is the context of the organisation, its past and present and its current challenges that define how foresight is used in practice. Pfeffer and Sutton (2006, p. 2) write: 'Instead of copying what others do, we should copy how they think'. The point is that using best practice copies a process and that's easy enough to do, whereas more value comes from understanding why people in successful organisations designed those processes the way they did, and that's a lot more difficult to discover.

Best practice is about using someone else's experience to inform your operations. It's only useful when there is a single right answer and that answer is accepted and unquestioned by people in the relevant field. With best practice, everyone has a shared understanding about the nature of the thing being 'best practiced'. Ways of knowing in the best practice space are also fixed. There are a set of often tacitly accepted ways of doing something. This is the space where we find conventional strategic planning, where the process is so formularised that developing a plan often seems more like a compliance exercise than a strategic process. This isn't the realm of foresight work where mostly we do not know what we do not know, there are no right answers and there is no accepted and unquestioned understanding of the likely impact of change shaping the future of our organisations.

Best practice is also falling out of favour in the mainstream business world. Goddard and Eccles (2013) describe best practice as a recipe for failure:

> *the single most value-destructive idea to have come out of business schools and management consultancies over the past 20 years. All they have achieved is to urge the laggards to catch up with the herd.*

They point out that failing organisations rely on benchmarks and best practice rather than imagining their own model of success. And Gary Hamel (2009) writes "Why are we so satisfied with 'best practice' when we should be inventing bold new practices?" Best practice lives in today, bold new practice emerges from thinking about change, its implications for your operations and how to respond. Best practice is based on what organisations have done in response to today's challenges and is unlikely to be replicable in that form when responding to challenges in the future. I'm not saying don't read reports of how others use foresight. I am saying don't follow their process blindly. It's a starting point only; you will always need to adapt it and redesign it to suit your organisation and recognise that its value may not last for long as the world changes and the best practice becomes obsolete.

Case Studies

People typically ask for case studies of successful foresight to use as proof of concept, proof that foresight is valuable, proof that it's worth their resources and time. They are asking me to assure them that someone else has used it successfully and they can too. On one level I understand this. For me however, this request is an indicator that the person in trapped in the data driven decision making world of today and not yet ready to use foresight. To these people I now say 'you are asking the wrong question. Ask me not what companies use foresight successfully. Instead ask me 'what's the best way to test foresight in my organisation?'

I have also been asked for another sort of case study when I have done sessional teaching. This is a case study that sets a hypothetical situation that asks students to interrogate it to identify challenges, mistakes, solutions, ways forward. I call this the MBA effect. A senior bank manager once told me that using case studies is how adults learn and I need to provide them. Thankfully, my sigh was inside my head. Like best practice, case studies reflect someone else's circumstance and issues. Working through them is about applying a tool or thinking to a situation that you may never encounter in that form. Similar maybe, but not your exact situation or your exact challenges.

There are no right answers, no formula or benchmark that will ensure you use foresight successfully. A case study approach may generate some scenarios for example, but they are artificial. Giving you a case study in a workshop to ponder over is unlikely to provide you with the thinking capacity you need to use foresight well in your organisation. It may allow you to consider what tools might be appropriate in a particular situation but it won't give you the 'right way' to use foresight in all situations. As with best practice, read case studies but don't expect to get a 'silver bullet' from them. There are none.

It often seems to me that people asking for case studies want me to say 'do it like this, approach it like this, apply this tool in this situation, and it will all work out'. To these people I now say 'I could describe to you some situations I've been in while I worked in organisations or other hypothetical situations and ask you to discuss what happened or what you would do in that situation. But that won't change your understanding of how best to use foresight in your organisation, just how you think one organisation might respond given its context and its challenges.' I lose most people in the room then and they usually leave me terrible student feedback, but that's okay. Those people aren't ready to use foresight yet.

For me, using foresight is personal. It's changing the way **you** think about the future. You can read and analyse all the case studies you want or follow best practice, but unless your foresight switch is turned on, you are applying conventional thinking to the future and that won't help you craft futures ready strategy.

Trusting Insight and Emergence

I learned about the value of foresight by using it - how to design processes that were effective, how to talk to people about it, how to communicate outcomes, how to present a case for the value of using foresight in strategic processes. My academic study in foresight provided the intellectual grounding I needed to do this well and to redesign processes in the room when they weren't working well. Every organisation I've worked with has received a tailored approach to some degree; I don't think I've ever designed the same foresight process twice. And I'm still learning, still building insight. I do know that using foresight with people who are affected by change every day has the effect of building understanding and appreciation of the value and importance of foresight to a greater degree than you will ever get from a written case study or following best practice guidelines. In my opinion.

It's not actually the foresight process that matters most in the long run, although processes must of course be well designed and executed. It's what you and others in organisations do with that process. It's how you design the process to gain commitment to using it on a continuing basis, to encourage many and deep strategic conversations, to challenge now unhelpful assumptions about work and organisations in the future, to trust emerging ideas and insights, and to reframe your strategy processes to enable foresight to be used well. Only you can do that based on your knowledge of your organisation today.

Using foresight is about engaging with such uncertainty that it usually produces those wicked strategic problems that have no easy answers, arising from contexts that may never have happened before. There is no rule book for unique situations – what was reasonable in the past and the present is unlikely to be reasonable or useful when you are facing the unknown. I see my role as giving you the ability to think about using foresight in practice in your context to face those wicked problems, not follow yesterday's rule book.

This book then provides you not with case studies or best practice examples. It provides instead a set of principles, concepts, frameworks, methods and reflections that you can use to design a foresight process that will be useful for your organisation and its challenges. Even with that set of resources though, you will need to learn to trust emerging insights that don't have the depth of data to meet today's validity requirements but may well hold the kernel of an idea critical for your organisation's future.

I admit that my resistance to providing case studies and best practice examples is a blindspot for me. It's one I've thought about a lot and one I've decided to keep. I also admit I'm asking you to trust me that using foresight in practice is valuable and only you can decide whether I've earned your trust. Read the book before you decide.

Why This Book?

One of my guiding principles since establishing Thinking Futures in 2007 has been to share information on what I know about using foresight as widely as I can. I wrote my three Strategic Futures Guides in 2007, 2009 and 2013 and my Reference Guide in 2015, I run webinars and share resources as part of how I enact this principle in my work. This book is published with a Creative Commons License so that it is accessible and usable in practice. I am also working to help people starting out with using foresight through my free membership program that I am now developing.

This book replaces my three existing Strategic Futures Guides:

- Using Futures Approaches: a guide to getting started,
- Environmental Scanning: what it is and how to do it, and
- Strategic Thinking: what it is and how to do it.

These guides had similar content, so it made sense to combine them to put everything you need to use foresight in your strategy development is in one book. Writing the book has also given me the opportunity to update and revise that content to include more recent research on foresight.

How the Book is Organised

The book takes you through the steps involved in using foresight in strategy processes and should ideally be read sequentially. That said, each chapter is more or less self-contained so you can explore topics of interest right now too.

Chapter 2 is about my foresight journey, how I started out, how I eventually moved to work full-time in the foresight field and some reflections on that experience so far. Here I'm aiming to show that it's possible to start using foresight with no prior knowledge as long as you are willing to establish a strong intellectual and methodological base as quickly as possible.

Chapter 3 provides a conceptual framework for using foresight and some basic foresight concepts and principles. Understanding what foresight is about and how to design processes that suit your organisation are prerequisites for successful implementation. Ken Wilber's integral theory and Richard Slaughter's social foresight model provide the conceptual framework.

Chapter 4 explores the relationship between foresight and strategy. It covers challenges with, and the need to reframe conventional strategic planning to use foresight in strategy development, and an overview of the four-stage strategy process to do that. This chapter also introduces the Generic Foresight Process Framework (Voros, 2003) and a summary of other foresight frameworks.

Chapter 5 identifies the preliminary steps you need to consider before infusing foresight into your strategy development processes. It covers an organisational futurist's audit to help you identify your positioning in your organisation, prerequisites for foresight use and the steps to take to begin using foresight.

Chapter 6 provides an overview of some foresight methods you can use in your organisation. Choosing methods carefully is essential because you have to match those methods to the foresight readiness of your organisation.

Chapter 7 covers how you do environmental scanning, the foundation for foresight infused strategy development. It takes you through the steps involved in scanning so you can identify change that matters for your organisation's future. It provides you with enough information to start doing scanning in your organisation.

Chapter 8 deals with strategic thinking, the core activity we engage in when we are using foresight in strategy development. This chapter provides an overview of what strategic thinking is, the differences between thinking and planning, being alert to your cognitive biases and getting started with strategic thinking.

Chapter 9 provides some of my lessons learned from my experience using foresight since 1999.

Chapter 10 is some final comments and some self-reflection questions for you.

2 My Foresight Journey

I was fortunate to be able to use foresight in the strategy processes of two universities – Swinburne University from 1999 to 2005 and at Victoria University (VU) from 2005 to 2007. My foresight journey is inextricably linked to the introduction of foresight at Swinburne and by the time I left to go to VU I was committed to the use of foresight in strategy development.

More than that though, I realised foresight was part of my worldview. I now can't imagine doing a job where I can't use foresight. This chapter gives you my story, how I learned about foresight, how I have used it and some reflections on my journey to date.

Learning about Foresight at Swinburne

I was called into the Vice-Chancellor's office one day in late 1998 – those of you who work in universities will know that this is always an interesting experience! At the time, I was working in the Higher Education Division looking after strategic, student and resource planning, but I was struggling with the University's approach to planning. You know what it's like: big document, lots of actions, lots of key performance indicators and a rigid process for reviewing it each year. It was a compliance exercise and seemed to have little to do with setting and achieving strategy.

I had started to talk about my misgivings but nothing much was happening – or so I thought. The Higher Education Division at the time was also under review, since there was a general perception that the Divisional

Office had too many administrative staff and was diverting resources away from teaching and research. This remains a common complaint in universities today!

I didn't know that at the time that the Vice-Chancellor and one of the Vice-Presidents had been at a British Council seminar on foresight in the United Kingdom. They saw its value and decided to bring foresight to Swinburne as part of the wider organisational changes being planned. My visit to the Vice-Chancellor's office was part of those changes. The conversation went something like this:

VC: We are re-structuring the Higher Education Divisional Office, and one of the jobs that will disappear is yours.
Maree (thinking): Okay, I knew that was coming. But, I think I'm okay.
VC: We are creating a new central planning office, and we would like you to manage it.
Maree: Okay, that would be great. Thank you.
VC: And we would like you to do foresight…
Maree (thinking): What on earth is foresight?
Maree: Okay, that sounds interesting. Do any other universities in Australia do foresight?
VC: No.
Maree: Okay, when do I start?

I went back to my office and looked up foresight on Google. My foresight journey had begun.

What on Earth Was I Doing?

I had achieved one thing – we could now change the way we did planning. But I had no idea what foresight was, no idea about how it might be useful for us or how to go about integrating it into a strategic planning process.

I was also going to have a new boss – another interesting experience. This would be my fourth job in eight years at Swinburne and while I was looking forward to the change, I was anxious about how on earth I could make foresight a reality when I knew so little about it. As an Enneagram Type 5, appearing competent in public is important to me so I searched out as much information as I could. If I was going to make sense to others, I had to at least have a reasonable understanding of what I was talking about.

The search was productive. While there was no other formal foresight program in an Australian university, many had used scenario thinking on an ad hoc basis. I began to gather a portfolio of information and ideas and started making contact with people online. I moved to my new boss's unit in early 1999 and we worked on how to implement a foresight program at Swinburne.

Now, I was to discover that my new boss and the Vice-Chancellor knew even less about the detail of foresight than I did, so my anxiety grew. I kept doing web searches, reading books, trying to find people who knew about foresight, looking frantically for anything that might help. I began to put together a paper for our planning committee about how we might move forward with a new planning framework that incorporated foresight. I decided that scenario thinking sounded like a good tool for us to use and suggested we involve staff in the process by getting them to participate in a foresight network. So far, so good.

I then discovered by accident that Richard Slaughter was coming to Swinburne to set up the Australian Foresight Institute. It is a characteristic of universities that I found this out from an external source, but when I mentioned it to my boss, he was happy to confirm it. The anxiety lessened a little, knowing there would be at least one person at Swinburne who really knew what foresight was all about.

Implementation Begins

In the latter half of 1999, after the luxury of six months immersing myself in the foresight literature, I moved to set up a foresight activity in the following ways:

- a discussion paper about developing a foresight capability at Swinburne which included the first draft of a foresight framework and the establishment of a Foresight Network of staff,
- a new planning framework, and
- planning for a pilot scenario thinking exercise in 2000.

The aim of using foresight stated in the discussion paper was:

to facilitate a shift in orientation from paper to people and to provide the context in which the organization, as a whole, can be more reflective about its future...[and] to present staff with an opportunity to be involved, if they wish, in the process of thinking through options for the University's future.

With the endorsement of my boss and the Vice-Chancellor, the paper was accepted. We had an expression of interest process for the Foresight Network with nominees approved by their managers to ensure that they would be given the time to participate. There was good interest and we had 10 staff, both academic and general, signed up by the end of 1999. I pursued the Network first because everything I had read had left me with the message that people throughout the organisation needed to be involved in foresight as well as senior managers.

During this time, I talked to people, attended countless meetings, wrote more reports, got trained in scenario thinking and started planning for the Horizon 20 scenario thinking exercise in 2000. I employed Joseph Voros as our first Strategic Foresight Analyst in 2000 and he began to develop what would end up as the Generic Foresight Process Framework (Voros, 2003). Joe's arrival signalled great relief for me as I was no longer alone and had a partner in foresight. One of the first things we did was develop our business idea using scenario planning methodology as shown in Figure 1 (Van der Heijden, 2005).

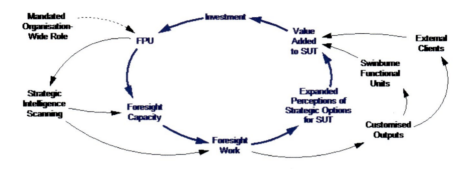

Figure 1: Original Swinburne Foresight Business Idea

This diagram gave us a framework for our role in the University, how we were going to demonstrate value, as well as identifying what our outputs would be – this was a top-level framework, the next job was to work on the detail.

A New Planning Framework

The University's strategic plan was due for review in 2000 so we had the opportunity to use the new planning framework that was underpinned by foresight. At the end of 2000, we produced a single page Statement of Direction 2010 that described the sort of organisation that Swinburne wanted to be and its defining characteristics in 2010. We also had several enabling plans to support the statement but the big, glossy plan was no more.

The Statement was our first foresight publication although it was not labelled as that and had not emerged from a university wide foresight process. The major benefit of the Statement was that it shifted the planning frame of reference out to ten years rather than the previous three to five years, and we began to see a corresponding shift in the thinking timeframe of staff. I was proud of this statement. Instead of asking people to read a conventional plan, we had a clear and concise statement of our preferred future and how we planned to get there on one page.

Horizon 20 Pilot Scenarios Project

We ran the Horizon 20 scenario process with a small group of staff including the Foresight Network, with senior managers attending at the beginning and the end of the workshop. These managers were invited to attend the two days of the workshop as their diaries permitted, but few took up that invitation.

The staff involved in this first workshop were enthusiastic in their response to the experience, but the managers were perplexed about the purpose and outcomes, and some were openly aggressive about how we were in their view, wasting their and our time. My first indication of the power of experiencing a foresight process, of the foresight switch being turned on, happened in the last session when one participant, in response to the managers' critique, said:

> *I wouldn't expect you to understand the value of the process we have been through over the past two days because you didn't go through that process yourself.*

We decided then that we would introduce scenario thinking at the unit level to build an understanding of its value among staff after they had experienced the process. We also decided that the University focused Swinburne Scenarios Project we were thinking about for 2002 needed to focus on senior managers rather than staff as was originally intended. The mangers needed to go through the process if the value of foresight as a tool and its outcomes were to be taken seriously and used in our ongoing strategy processes.

Unfortunately, the Foresight Network floundered in 2001 because it was difficult for staff to meet often enough as the entire group and as expected, it was clear that scenarios produced by staff in the Horizons 20 exercise were not regarded as having enough credibility to be used in university planning activities. We gathered feedback about their perceptions of the Network members' experience and involvement in the Network:

- incredible time deficit was a real issue,
- general interest in both foresight and the professional development opportunity it affords,
- wanting to "make a real difference" as opposed to being window dressing,
- enthusiasm for the idea of foresight, tempered by fatigue and cynicism of 'senior management's motives', and
- wanting to be a part of positive change, both in the organisation and society.

The feedback suggested that the concept of a network was a good one but that it lacked support from managers for people to be involved. It was perhaps an idea whose time had not yet come at Swinburne.

Introducing Foresight

A series of Introduction to Foresight workshops for University units were designed by Joseph Voros and delivered during 2001. These aimed to introduce staff to foresight, its intellectual base in futures studies and how it linked to strategy development. This seminar and a foresight primer publication became part of the University's online induction process.

We also began to run workshops that were introductions to scenario thinking and involved preparing what we called 'learning scenarios.' The workshops were not intended to produce scenarios which could be used, but rather were intended to provide staff with the experience of using scenario thinking as a way of thinking about the future. Our learnings from these workshops resulted in a series of three workshops being developed and refined: Learning Scenarios, an introduction to scenario thinking; Exploratory Scenarios, developing scenarios around a particular issue; and Strategic Implications, a follow-on from Exploratory Scenarios which considered strategic options.

The outcomes from this initial work were limited, but evaluation indicated that approximately 90% of those attending the first type of workshop would have been happy to use scenario thinking in their own unit planning and commented that the workshop:

- brought into sharper focus the existence and relevance of thinking about 'plausibilities',
- explained the practical implications of foresight,
- gave examples that put into practice what needs to happen, and
- gave a good framework for strategic thinking.

These comments sounded like we had met our objectives in running these workshops and gave us hope that the foresight message was spreading.

We also produced monthly email Foresight Snippets which contained items of interesting, challenging and sometimes weird information that might or might not have been directly relevant to Swinburne. The Snippets focused on the broad social environment while *prospect,* the quarterly Foresight Bulletin, provided information about education related developments and futures work. *prospect* was focused around the University's five strategic themes and developments in each of these broad areas. Both the Snippets and *prospect* were designed to be conversation starters for ongoing strategic conversations.

A reader survey of the Foresight Snippets indicated that 74% of readers found them useful and informative, with 38% of readers seeking more futures-oriented items. *prospect* was used in the development of one of the strategic plans for The Entrepreneurial University strategic theme. The Foresight Seminars were successful, with 100% of attendees indicating they now understood the concept, 95% wanting to find out more, and approximately 85% willing to use it in their unit planning.

I described our implementation process like this (Conway 2001):

> *Our approach has been to describe foresight as a process, best understood by experiencing it. We are focusing on one methodology to ensure a simple framework for implementation and understanding. We have a five-year plan to embed scenario planning in the University which may be optimistic, but our initial, limited efforts have been received positively by participants.*

This sounded like we knew what we were doing and that there was an accepted process. Then I explained the implementation context:

> *The introduction of foresight into [Swinburne's] planning processes at a time of considerable organisational and cultural change is problematic, not only because it is yet one more change staff have to consider, but also because it bears little overt relationship yet to the day-to-day work of individual units and benefits cannot be quantitatively measured. We are therefore operating in an environment where skepticism about the value of foresight in general ... is high, but where there is, mostly, a*

commensurately high degree of tolerance until the results are known.

I don't think the situation we found ourselves in when we were introducing foresight would be that different to what organisations are facing now. Details will differ but what we did and what you will be doing is working to integrate a new approach into an existing strategy process in an organisation that is already changing in significant ways. You will be asking people to challenge their assumptions about the future as well as deal with what's going on in the present. No one will thank you for that. In hindsight though, I can say that while challenging for me as a foresight novice, the experience helped me learn how best to introduce foresight into an organisation and to see firsthand what happens when the foresight switch is turned on.

During 2002, Joe left the Unit to work as an academic with Richard Slaughter in the Swinburne foresight program. Marcus Barber took his place as the Strategic Foresight Analyst, so I still had a partner in foresight!

Organisational Politics

During all this activity, I was naively unaware about the depth of organisational politics that would ultimately result in the demise of foresight at the university. My boss was not liked by other senior managers and they may have had good reasons for that. My experience though was working with someone who trusted me to get on with the job and was always available to have a conversation in which I was both challenged and supported. I was to discover that because of their dislike of my boss, these very smart people decided at the outset that this foresight thing was not going to succeed. They would never give it a chance.

I now understand that their resistance wasn't necessarily because they thought using foresight was a bad idea. Rather they decided that they would not support it because they didn't like my boss and had not been involved in the decision to introduce foresight (although not being involved in decision making was not unusual at the time). I learned all this in subsequent conversations with these managers, with whom I had always worked well in the past but with whom my relationship deteriorated as I worked hard to use foresight at Swinburne.

Their resistance ranged from jokes about the word foresight, passive refusal to be involved, being told by a Pro Vice-Chancellor that she was only talking to me out of goodwill and that I should look for another job because foresight wasn't going to succeed, to being told that when I worked in the faculties everyone liked and respected me but people no longer trusted me and didn't understand why I was doing what I was doing. I did have one smug moment however. After Joe and I had delivered a presentation on foresight at Swinburne to the annual meeting with the federal government education department, a Pro Vice-Chancellor announced that she saw no value in foresight and that it had no connection to her day to today work. The Vice-Chancellor remained silent but to my delight, the government departmental secretary liked it so much he invited us to present to his managers group in Canberra.

Now I understand why they reacted like this. In these early days though, I had no idea of this danger lurking beneath the organisational surface, and what I now see as my naivety at understanding organisational politics didn't help me grasp the reality that was all around me. Fortunately, there were many other people at the University who were more open and more willing to tolerate using foresight to see if there was value for Swinburne.

A New Leader: Killing Foresight Softly

That a new Vice-Chancellor would arrive at Swinburne at some stage in 2004 was known for some time. One of my responses to this was to develop a 'convince the new VC' strategy around the value of foresight as a strategy development tool. We did a five-year review of foresight at Swinburne which reminded us of how far we had come since 1999 and how close we were to embedding foresight into our strategy development.

Within months of the new Vice-Chancellor arriving however, it was clear he wasn't interested, and his lack of interest was perhaps more obvious than that of the senior managers. This was a closed mind I was dealing with, someone who apparently knew little about using foresight and because it appeared not to fit his worldview or his plan for Swinburne, there was no engagement. None. I was talking to the proverbial brick wall. He may of course recall this time differently and instead simply saw me as someone with organisational baggage he could do without. And that's fair enough.

Even as I was making what turned out to be a last desperate pitch, the following indicators that foresight was doomed were clear:

- the swiftness with which some senior managers called for the removal of my boss from his position (I have no idea what they said about my role but can imagine!),
- the removal of the term foresight from all planning documentation, including removal of associated terminology such as environmental scanning,
- initial agreement to use inclusive approaches such as surveying staff about their views of the future of Swinburne prior to strategy being developed, that turned into the Vice-Chancellor effectively doing my job for me by running the planning process himself,

- reactions to my suggestions that the Vice-Chancellor might like to read our scanning reports to inform his thinking about future options turned out to be one of those 'oops' moments when he responded with words along the lines of 'I don't need anything like that to inform my thinking', and
- his review of the University Planning Framework that eliminated all foresight elements.

It eventually dawned on me that my commitment to using foresight approaches in my work was not shared by the new Vice-Chancellor and I had to leave Swinburne. I have always believed that I wanted to leave a job before someone told me I've passed my use-by date and I could now see very clear signs. I proposed that over time I move out of the Director position so the Vice-Chancellor could implement the new framework without me nagging him about foresight. His proposed review of the planning unit would also be easier for him to do if I wasn't the Director. I moved to a new position on the unstated understanding that I would leave Swinburne as soon as was reasonable, which I serendipitously did within a few months.

At Victoria University

I presented foresight up front when I applied for my job at Victoria University and to their credit, they indicated that while they didn't really understand what it was, they were willing to give it a go. I was more cautious here, introducing foresight in different ways and operating for some time in what I call stealth mode, trying to use foresight without anyone noticing. I did scenario workshops and started to work with units on scanning. A Strategic Analyst was employed at the same time as me to help with the scanning but ended up being immersed in data analysis.

Despite my efforts, foresight falling of the priority list turned out to be the hallmark of my time at VU.

After working with departments, I ran a university wide scenario thinking workshop in 2007. It was open to all staff, designed as a taster, an introduction to foresight. There was strong attendance and the feedback was good. I also helped the VU Futures team with environmental scanning – this project was set up shortly after the workshop and I continued to work with the team after I had started Thinking Futures. This group of people were smart, open thinkers and their strategic scans were some of the best I've seen. The project disappeared when this Vice-Chancellor left unfortunately, another example of the fragility of foresight work that is not well embedded in an organisation and dependent on individuals for survival.

My role here was similar to that at Swinburne so the challenge of integrating foresight while balancing strategic planning, government reporting, quality management and government audits, student surveys, data analysis and reporting, managing a wonderful group of 20 staff and a unit restructure was very familiar. It eventually proved too much for me though. I decided that I'd have to leave VU and the best boss I think I've had if I was to pursue using foresight full-time.

When I said this to the Vice-Chancellor finally, she told me I had to stay until the end of the year and finish the things I'd started. She told my boss to do whatever it took. This was a first since you are usually just waved goodbye when you say you are resigning from a university job. Mouth agape, I went part-time and set up Thinking Futures while helping the VU Futures team.

Some Reflections

During my foresight journey I came to realise that one of the biggest gaps in our political frameworks, in our social norms and assumptions about the future and in how organisations develop strategy is the capacity to think in a deeper, more reflective, meaningful and systematic way about the future. This gap became my mission: to help people use foresight in practice and change the way they think about the future, and to embed its use into organisational strategy development.

On another level, the power of being part of a foresight experience – what I described earlier as the foresight switch coming on - has stayed with me since my time at Swinburne. At foresight's core lies human agency. It's people using foresight to think differently, to see new ways of working that will engender change in our strategy development and increase our future readiness. The walk in, walk out speaker/expert/facilitator will present interesting information and processes, but the ability of people to design and participate in their own foresight process will result in more compelling outcomes for their organisations as individual and collective thinking about possible futures expands beyond the status quo.

Why do I care so much about using foresight in practice? If we take a global perspective, there is much to be hopeful about in the future, but so much more that makes us pause and wonder how we can go on this way without changing some fundamental beliefs about how we live, work, and relate to each other and the planet on which we live. Our worldviews, the set of beliefs upon which we base our decisions and make sense of the world, are not fixed and are often constraining as we face the future. Our ability to believe we are totally right in the face of disconfirming evidence that challenges our worldviews is unfortunately very strong.

We can change our worldviews. We can challenge and reframe them as the world changes around us. In my work, I sometimes run an exercise called *Advice from the Future* and ask people to imagine themselves in the same place doing the same thing but in 10 or 20 years. Then, I ask them to take the role of good ancestors and give advice to their descendants in the room today. Advice about what they should know about the future, about what they need to pay attention to today and advice about what they need to stop doing. It's always an insightful process.

Some people struggle with the flipped thinking that is asked of them, but ultimately the advice provided can be applied today to start moving beyond the status quo, to start understanding how changing how we think about the future is so important. People alternatively think it's a fun or pointless process but when we discuss it, most people in the room get the point that they were giving advice to themselves without the constraints of today at play. There are new ways to think about our challenges today.

One thing that made a difference for me was at the end of my first year in the Strategic Foresight course at Swinburne, when we were asked to reflect on what struck us most strongly during the year. I said without thinking (which is most unusual for me) "that we are responsible for future generations". I wasn't sure where that had come from but I knew then that I had accepted that responsibility. Something had shifted in my brain. Thinking about the future had rewired my brain and my worldview. And if you and I aren't responsible for future generations, who is?

The future we are creating today is ultimately for our descendants. Every decision we make as individuals and organisations has impacts that flow downstream into the future. Flipping our perspective away from seeing the future from today's perspective to being good ancestors moves us beyond thinking the future will be more of today to open up new ways of thinking about change and how we will respond in the present.

Iain Wallace, the Swinburne Vice-Chancellor who told me to 'do foresight' was a visionary and prepared to move Swinburne beyond the status quo even if people didn't like it. He recognised the value of foresight and gave me the opportunity to surface and use my own foresight capacity. Liz Harman was the VU Vice-Chancellor who gave me the space and resources to use foresight and was smart enough to recognise its value to her in her redesign of VU planning. That suited me. An open mind is all that is needed.

Once your foresight capacity is surfaced and used in practice, there is no going back to conventional thinking and conventional strategy development - and that is a good thing. I shall be forever grateful to these two Vice-Chancellors for starting me on my foresight journey.

3 A Conceptual Framework

One of the mistakes I made when I was a foresight novice was to begin using foresight without any clear intellectual framework to guide my work. Reading books was not enough. Combined with the negative impact of organisational politics it meant that successful implementation at Swinburne was always going to be difficult – but this understanding was only apparent in hindsight! The foresight field has an emerging, strong conceptual basis which you need to understand first if you are to run successful processes and get the outcomes you need. This chapter provides first some foresight principles and core concepts and then a conceptual framework to help you design how to infuse foresight into your strategy approaches. Hopefully my lessons learned will make your path a little easier.

Foresight Principles

Using foresight processes can look deceptively simple. There are however, a set of foresight principles common to all good foresight work even though there is no universal agreement about how they are described or understood. Ask a group of futurists and foresight practitioners what they think these principles are and you will get a long list and much discussion about definitions. Here are the principles I use in my work.

The future does not yet exist. Foresight explores ideas about and images of the future. There are no data about the future and relying on extrapolating what we know about the present is seldom useful for strategy. Today's data are essential but so are our imaginations about the possible that doesn't exist yet – images and ideas about what matters that are informed by knowledge, experience and expertise are a valid data source.

The future is not predetermined, inevitable or fixed. There are always alternative futures. Conventional planning approaches assume a single linear future and result in 'bet the farm' strategies, the equivalent to crossing your fingers and hoping you are right. Using foresight allows the range of alternative futures always available to an organisation to be explored **before** strategy is developed.

The future is uncertain and not predictable – we have choices today. I have an almost visceral reaction when I see the word prediction and those annual lists of what **will** happen next year. Predictions are invariably extrapolations of today, based on what we believe we know today. Attempting to predict the future can result in smart people making statements that turn out to be a bit silly in hindsight as I highlighted in the Introduction. Taking time to think about implications of change for your organisation will engender sensemaking that lets you move beyond prediction and engage with future uncertainty.

There are different types of futures whether preposterous, potential, possible, plausible and preferable. Using foresight in strategy development usually focuses on the preferable future, the one that provides the long- term context to guide action and decision making today. You will arrive at an understanding of what that is however, only by working through the other types of futures first, reducing the scale as your understanding of what matters for your organisation increases in depth. See the next section *Different Types of Futures* for more information.

Futures outcomes can be influenced by our action or inaction today. We can and should take action to move towards a preferred future or to mitigate an undesirable future. Inaction however, means ending up in someone else's future and in that case, you have no option but to deal with whatever you get. Inaction leads inevitably to being surprised when change you thought was highly improbable becomes a reality.

We are all responsible for future generations – every decision made today affects them. For me, this principle is the most critical when doing foresight work. We use foresight in strategy development to craft robust strategy today *and* to ensure we do no harm to future generations. The two are not mutually exclusive.

Different Types of Futures

The futures cone presents the idea that there is always more than one future in graphic form (Figure 2). A brief description of each type of future follows.

All futures after today are **potential**, latent events that can happen and human capacities that can be developed.

Preposterous futures are just that - preposterous given the time frame for which we are developing strategy. Preposterous futures are definitely worth exploring to stretch thinking into that realm of the truly weird and strange, but preposterous is likely to be of little use in your strategy development today. Their value lies in helping us think very long term where there just could be a kernel of something that triggers an idea that might be useful today.

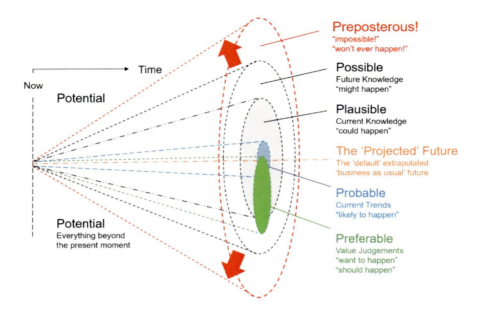

Figure 2: Futures Cones (this version copyright Joseph Voros, 2013)

All futures after today are **potential**, latent events that can happen and human capacities that can be developed.

Preposterous futures are just that - preposterous given the time frame for which we are developing strategy. Preposterous futures are definitely worth exploring to stretch thinking into that realm of the truly weird and strange, but preposterous is likely to be of little use in your strategy development today. Their value lies in helping us think very long term where there just could be a kernel of something that triggers an idea that might be useful today.

The **projected** future is likely to be the one in your current strategic plan: the official future, the single future. This is the future we need to test and challenge for future validity and relevance by using foresight.

Possible futures might happen, but we don't have the knowledge right now to make them happen. I used to say that Star Trek was a good example of possible futures. When I started using foresight the idea of transporting people intact from one place to another and using mobile communication devices didn't really seem likely in the short term (remember I started using foresight in pre iPhone days!). Both are now a reality or likely to become a reality. Never dismiss the possible future without exploring its implications first, because it can become reality more quickly than you think.

Probable futures are the ones that are based on trends so strong that they are likely to happen in the timeframe you are exploring for your strategy. In scenario thinking, these are called predetermined elements, things you take into account in every scenario you develop.

Plausible futures are what you explore in strategy work since the aim is to develop futures ready strategy that informs action today. These have to be plausible for people to be able to draw on them today. They are futures that are based on knowledge we currently have **and** our understanding of how that knowledge will evolve over the next 10-20 years.

Preferable futures are where you end up by using foresight in your strategy work. This is the strategic destination that you put into you plan and use as your reference point for decision making today. You explore possible, plausible, probable and preposterous futures first, looking for the thread that you can follow back to design your preferred future today.

Knowing which space you are in when using foresight is important. My view of the value of the Futures Cone is that it allows us to explore the possible and probable and even the preposterous before narrowing our lens to focus on plausible and preferred. Working only in the plausible and preferred spaces without exploring probable and possible, and even preposterous first means that you will be creating strategy on what you know today and what is very likely to be in place in the near future. You will be starting from today and extrapolating out, taking today's assumptions into the future, rather than exploring broadly what might be in the future and then using insights that emerge to inform your strategy today.

Short and Long-Term Thinking

In most conventional strategic plans, the 'future' is around five years away and therefore short term in nature. Foresight approaches use a longer term 10 to 20-year timeframe to facilitate thinking that moves beyond the boundaries of convention and today. It can however, be quite difficult for people to deal with much beyond the short term future if minds are focused on the tangible work on their desks and for whatever reason, closed to the potential of what might happen. If people are overwhelmed with the busyness of today, they will usually not be able to see a space in their schedules or their brains to be able to devote time to thinking about change and its implications, particularly if they can't see how it will help them do their work right now.

Yet thinking about the long term may is urgent. In the long run, it doesn't really matter how well you deal with what is perceived to be urgent today if your organisation doesn't exist in the future. The reality is that if you spend time thinking about the long term, today's urgencies will become less urgent and you will be able to see what is important. I can write this because I have experienced this shift in perspective. The long term does provide a context for decision making today and lets you focus on what really matters for your organisation.

Whether intentional or not, short term thinking also allows people to remain within their comfort zones where there is much data, where assumptions aren't challenged and where historical success provides safety. In this zone it's possible for people to subconsciously convince themselves that the future will be more of the same in order to cope with what's going on around them. But, innovative thinking and futures ready strategy does not emerge from comfort zones. I sometimes hear people in workshops say that they are happy in their comfort zones, to which I always say that being happy in your comfort zone is a dangerous place to be with disruptive change all around your organisation.

Reliance on data driven or evidence based decision making also exacerbates our inability to deal with more than the short term. There are no data about the future, crystal balls don't work and we can't predict the future except by luck, no matter what anyone says and how hard we try to convince ourselves we can. Those wedded to data and evidence as the primary basis for decision making will generally have a difficult time seeing any value in exploring the future, yet as Ian Wilson a US scenario thinker says (Wilson 2006):

> However good our futures research may be, we shall never be able to escape from the ultimate dilemma that all our knowledge is about the past, and all our decisions are about the future.

There are no future facts. Applying past and present knowledge to the future may once have been enough for strategy development, but that approach has very limited value today.

This is why 10-20 years in the minimum time frame for foresight work. Taking people away from the conceivable present stretches thinking and takes them into spaces where new thinking can emerge. The constraints of the present are removed, it's demonstrated that many assumptions are no longer useful and people have permission to think in new ways about their work and their organisation. This is still uncomfortable because it's an unfamiliar thinking space but that's okay. A success factor in my foresight work is whether one of more participants say 'my brain hurts' or something similar at some stage during the project or workshop. This is not a bad thing; it's a sign that their thinking is being stretched beyond the conventional.

We need to be clear about the timeframe in which we are operating when using foresight because that will influence both the choice of methods and the outcomes achieved, as well as the degree to which participants think in new ways about the future or whether they remain trapped in the present. The time frame you choose for foresight work must however, always be 10 years or more.

Challenging Assumptions

One of the hidden obstacles in using foresight or even using a method on a single occasion, is that you will be challenging the existing state of affairs, both in terms of where the organisation is, what it does today and how people think about the future of their organisation. While the past and present will undoubtedly shape the future to some degree and some artifacts from the past and the present will persist into the future, what we see as reasonable and true today is unlikely to be seen as reasonable or true in the future. Basing our decisions about the unknown and uncertain future on information only from the past and the present will result in strategy that fails when it meets the future. This is why you will need to work continuously on surfacing and challenging assumptions about how the future might evolve.

Hines (2003) writes that while "futures work is really all about challenging worldviews or epistemologies … the number of organizations, particularly corporations, intellectually ready for this is very, very small." At the heart of this lack of foresight readiness is the inability to challenge assumptions. Unquestioned assumptions constrain the degree of openness of an organisation to new information and new methods of strategy development. Think here about companies like Borders, Blockbuster and Kodak. Smart people, good business models when established and once leaders in their fields. When the world changed around them however, people in leadership roles were closed to seeing external disruption to their operating environment as a real threat, leading eventually to their demise.

Influencing strategic decision making processes is the ultimate aim of using foresight but influencing the minds and assumptions of people who make those decisions will come first. It wasn't changes in their external environments that destroyed Borders, Blockbuster and Kodak. It was the inability of leaders to move beyond the status quo in their thinking and accept disconfirming evidence that challenged their beliefs about their businesses, to consider discontinuous or disruptive change as real threats to their business models. They fell prey to their cognitive biases and were trapped in the past by their assumptions. It is how leaders choose to respond to change, how open their minds are to new thinking and how good they are at bringing their people with them into the future that is one of the characteristics of successful organisations today.

A Word about Worldviews

To challenge assumptions effectively, you will need to first reflect on your worldview – how you create meaning from your experience of the world, how you filter events, what you accept to 'real' and what you dismiss as irrelevant or rubbish. Our brains are covert supporters in maintaining our assumptions because they operate as pattern recognition machines. They attempt to deal with new information by matching what they are seeing or hearing to what they have seen or heard before. They look for patterns and tend to ignore things that don't fit those patterns.

When confronted with the uncertainty and unknowable that characterises the future, our brains use our existing benchmarks of what we believe to be right and wrong, how things work, what is real and what it not to decide whether or not to let the new information in. Unless our foresight switches are turned on, our brains will encourage us to retreat to explanations based on what is already known. We will reject the new and the strange and fall into a certainty trap that does us no favours when we are dealing with the future.

When using foresight, you will be making a subjective assessment of the value of what you are finding about change, both indicators that are strong and weaker signals at the periphery. Being alert to ensure your mind doesn't retreat to validity assessments based on existing thinking patterns is essential. If not alert to your worldview when using foresight, you will miss things that just might be important, and you will make assumptions that may be just plain wrong. When this happens, I call it hitting an assumption wall - brick walls in your thinking that prevent you from surfacing, challenging and testing your assumptions about how you see the world, and what you believe to be true and right.

Using foresight is about thinking in new ways about existing and potential markets, competitors, social needs, political shifts, emerging technologies and new business models. It is about looking beyond current ways of working and thinking the unthinkable to see what might be needed in the future. It's the opposite of deciding strategy by starting with your existing capabilities, resources and perceived customer needs. Using foresight means your starting point is at least possible futures where you explore how your organisation can be successful in those futures and identify implications for today's strategy. Different thinking modes and worldviews are needed in each of these spaces. To face the future in any meaningful way you need to challenge your assumptions and build new thinking patterns. Foresight processes when done well will help you do that.

A Conceptual Framework for Foresight

The foresight field is still emerging as is its theoretical base. There is continuing discussion around the need to connect well developed practice such as scenario thinking with theory. Rohrbeck et al. (2015) identify three areas where the field is not yet well developed: ambiguous terminology, a weakly organised academic field and weak linkages to debates in general management journals. I won't get into that discussion here because it could be a book on its own, except to point out a recent development.

Foresight as **anticipation** is about viewing the future as part of the present, not some amorphous space that can't be defined and that is easy to ignore. More importantly perhaps, anticipating the future is about being reflexive – the ability to recognise the impact of your values, beliefs, mental models and cognitive biases on the way you make sense of the world today and how you craft the future.

When I first read papers on the discipline of anticipation, I did wonder about the degree of difference between foresight and anticipation. I'm open to being convinced of that difference, because the term anticipation does seem to more accurately reflect from where thinking in new ways about the future emerges – that is, the act of facing and anticipating the future in the present. The similarities and differences between how foresight and anticipation are understood will continue to be clarified since the domain where we try to make sense of how we think about the future is a dynamic one. I do have a sense though that talking about 'using foresight to anticipate the future' has the potential to become 'just the way we develop strategy around here'.

My Conceptual Base

This section provides an overview of the conceptual models I use to design my foresight work. These have helped me design processes and ways to help people move beyond the conventional in their thinking about the future. Richard Slaughter (2004) and Ken Wilber (2001) provide different models that when used alone or combined, create a strong conceptual framework that has informed my thinking about how to introduce foresight into an organisation's existing strategy process.

Slaughter's Social Foresight

Richard Slaughter developed the concept of a social foresight capacity and was instrumental in establishing the concept of Integral Futures in the foresight field. Slaughter's social foresight model demonstrates how society can move from a past-driven to a futures responsive culture. His five level model recognises that the development of a social foresight capacity will not occur in the near future and instead will be built up over a period of time. A description of those five levels follows.

Level 1: recognition that foresight is an innate human capacity: at this level a person's foresight capacity is often sub-conscious, and is used to make decisions about the future with little reflection or consideration of the processes in action. Individuals recognising and surfacing their capacity is the first step in the development of social foresight. At this level, using foresight is a solitary activity.

Level 2: a foresight discourse emerges: this level is reached when foresight ideas, concepts and approaches begin to be discussed by individuals who recognise and are using their own foresight capacity. As more and more people become familiar with and use the concepts, the validity of foresight work grows and a foresight discourse develops. It's at this level that our foresight capacities begin to be activated as a collective capacity.

Level 3: foresight methods begin to be used and increase analytic power: - this occurs when organisations are using foresight tools and methodologies in a range of ways. Using foresight has become collaborative and is the norm for strategy development.

Level 4: foresight processes, projects & structures embodied in variety of contexts - this level is reached when an organisation routinely uses foresight approaches to underpin its strategy development and has a permanent, customised foresight function.

Level 5: social foresight and long term thinking is the norm - is reached when a foresight capacity has developed across organisations and long term thinking to is the social norm - much like how we regard strategic planning now. At this stage, the use of foresight is overt, collective and supported by systemic processes in all organisations, government, business and education.

The power of this idea of the development of a social foresight capacity is that it highlights two things: first, the need to start with both individuals and groups when introducing foresight into an organisation and second, it is a developmental process. For example, you won't be able to start at Level 3 and expect success if you haven't first addressed Levels 1 and 2.

Wilber's Integral Four Quadrants

Ken Wilber's work in field of human consciousness generated his integral theory, a bringing together of the world's great historical, psychological, philosophical and spiritual traditions. Slaughter (2004, p. 152) describes his theory as an attempt to "honor all truths and acknowledge the value of different ways of knowing across all significant fields." And Voros (2003) writes:

> *Integral Futures ... does not take a singular perspective; rather it recognizes a plurality of perspectives. It is not confined to a single tool or methodology rather it is aware of the existence of an entire (indeed, infinite) tool kit. It recognizes that there are many ways of knowing - many paradigms, practices and methodologies of knowledge seeking - and that no single paradigm can be assigned pre-eminence ... Integral Futures Studies welcomes, embraces and values all careful and sincere approaches to knowledge-seeking in all sphere of human activity to which they are both appropriate and adequate - including analytical rationality, intuitive insight and spiritual inspiration.*

I mentioned in the Acknowledgements that integral theory informs how I design my work projects – I use the four quadrant framework to do this (Wilber 2001). The four quadrants provide a more comprehensive way of viewing the reality for which we are developing strategy by integrating both internal and external perspectives on both an individual and collective level. The framework consists of a two-by-two matrix - interior and exterior and individual and collective - which creates four quadrants to explore: interior/individual, exterior/individual, interior/collective and exterior/collective as shown in Figure 3.

The **Lower Left** quadrant is the cultural, inter-subjective realm, where only the group can provide interpretation of meaning. This is the space where the 'rules of the game' by which individuals come together and co-exist are shared. The validity claim in this quadrant is *justness*.

Wilber's Four Quadrants

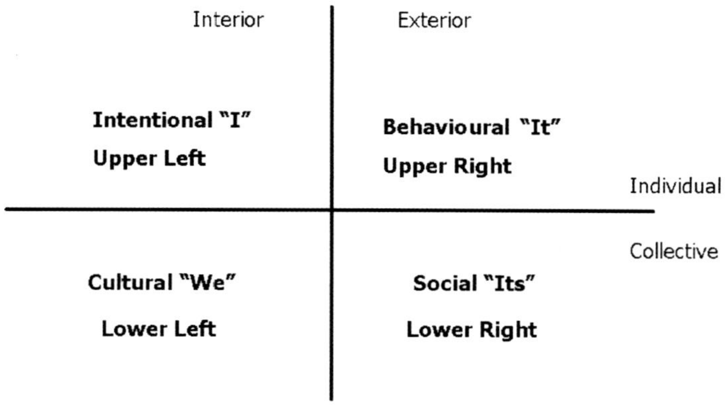

Interior	Exterior
Intentional "I"	**Behavioural "It"**
Upper Left	**Upper Right**
	Individual
	Collective
Cultural "We"	**Social "Its"**
Lower Left	**Lower Right**

Figure 3: Wilber's Four Quadrant Model

The **Upper Right** quadrant is the objective realm of individual and organisational behaviour, with a validity claim of *truth*, while the **Lower Right** quadrant is the inter-objective social realm, the world external to the individual or the organisation. The validity claim here is *functional fit*. The quadrants are interdependent, and tensions exist between them, such as tensions between individual and organisational or cultural values.

The different types of validity claim relate to different types of knowledge held in each quadrant. Accessing left hand quadrant knowledge always involves interpretation to make meaning visible, while right hand quadrant knowledge is empirical and is therefore already visible. Because each quadrant provides its own 'way of knowing' about a given reality or context, all four quadrants must be addressed when considering, for example, an organisational issue, paradox or strategic challenge.

Looking at only the external and empirical quadrants and paying less or no attention to internal and interpretative will undermine your use of foresight in strategy development. Our thinking about the future happens in the Upper Left and is influenced by the organisational culture in the Lower Left. Designing Upper Right processes to respond to Lower Right change without taking the left-hand quadrants into account means processes may change but how people think about the organisation's future and whether the organisation lets in new information will probably not change. An integral framework for strategy development integrates both internal and external quadrants and sees knowledge that can be gleaned from each as valid sources of data.

Wilber's integral theory is significantly more complex than just the four quadrants and consists of concepts such as holons, lines or streams, states, waves and types found in each quadrant. More recent research has deepened understanding by identifying two ways to interrogate each quadrant – from a first person and a third person perspective which provide essentially different ways of knowing. This creates eight zones across the quadrants as described by Esbjorn-Hargens (2009):

> *These eight zones comprise what integral theory calls integral methodological pluralism (IMP), which includes such approaches as phenomenology (an exploration of first-person subjective realities), ethnomethodology (an exploration of second-person intersubjective realities), and empiricism (an exploration of third-person empirical realities).*

Integral Theory is an interesting and challenging space to explore within or outside of the strategy context. Esbjorn-Hargens'overview of Integral Theory discusses its complexity as clearly as anyone I have found so far. I have not yet moved beyond the four quadrants in my practice and that's the framework I use in the next section.

Bringing Slaughter and Wilber Together

Slaughter's social foresight development model can be adapted to describe the stages of development of an organisational foresight capacity. His five levels indicate clearly that developing a foresight capacity will not occur without some effort and without the involvement of many people. Indeed, Slaughter's model makes the critical observation that the ability to think about the future and thereby use our foresight capacities is innate and held by everyone. In an organisational sense, this reminds us that all staff have the ability to think strategically about the future as long as there are collective processes and a shared information base in place – these two things are the foundation that will enable a collective strategic foresight capacity to emerge.

The value of Wilber's framework for strategy development then lies in its basic premise that all four quadrants must be considered to understand how change might shape organisational futures. More than that, change in one quadrant needs to be reflected to the same degree in the other three quadrants if the desired organisational impact is to be achieved. The framework therefore validates data sourced from both the interior/individual quadrants - what goes on in our heads and our consciousness - and data located in the exterior/collective quadrant – what is happening within and external to our organisations. Indeed, Wilber suggests that without exploring all four quadrants, our understanding of a phenomenon or in our case resulting strategy, is always flawed.

Bringing Slaughter's levels and Wilber's quadrants together into a single conceptual model is shown in Figure 4. The development of a strategic foresight capacity is not linear, stages overlap and are continuous, as indicated by the cyclical nature of the arrows.

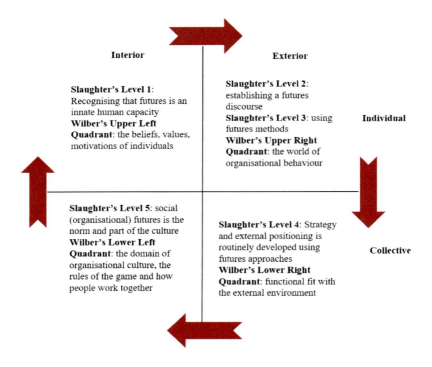

Figure 4: Bringing Slaughter and Wilber Together

From my experience, the general flow of development is:

- individuals overtly recognise their foresight capacities after being exposed to foresight concepts, and are supported to develop those capacities with training and resources,
- then, processes are put in place to enable an organisational conversation about using foresight to develop, which enables the use of foresight methods and tools in strategy development, so that
- over time, using foresight becomes embedded in strategy development to the degree where it can't be removed easily, and
- finally, organisational culture is underpinned by long term thinking generated from using futures approaches which in turn, reinforces the need for individuals to reflect on and build their own foresight capacities.

Using this combined framework, strategy development needs to take into account the following four types of 'data':

- **Upper Left**: Individual/Interior: understanding the inner motivations, beliefs and values of individual people, where images of the future are generated and held,
- **Upper Right**: Individual/Exterior: designing organisational foresight processes where images of the future are contested during strategy processes, and where preferred futures are designed and implemented,
- **Lower Left**: Collective/Interior: understanding the culture of an organisation, the space where the undiscussables live, where the 'rules' that determine whose image of the future is dominant can be found, and
- **Lower Right**: Collective/Exterior: understanding the nature of change happening in the organisation's social ecosystem.

This combined approach helps your organisation develop a strong organisational foresight capacity to use in your strategy development. If your organisation: (i) looks for both short and long-term change shaping its future on a continuing basis, (ii) enables people to think openly about the future, (iii) supports a culture that allows that thinking to be surfaced and used in strategy development, and (iv) designs collective and inclusive processes to explore alternative futures, identify strategic options and take action today, you will have a future facing organisation.

How I use the combined framework

When I start a new relationship with a client, I spend a little time with them to identify where they are in terms of their futures readiness. I use the four quadrants for this, and it doesn't really take much time to identify the gaps where foresight approaches can help. People I work with are ready to shift their thinking and they know their organisations need to change how they operate so I usually have quite open conversations that help me to identify how they can start using foresight effectively.

It's probably not a surprise after reading this far in the chapter that the gaps are generally in the left hand quadrants. The focus of conventional strategic planning lies in the right hand quadrants and pays little if any real attention to the left hand quadrants. It can be a difficult but not impossible task to help people move into the left hand quadrant space and it can be even more difficult to keep them engaged in that space once they are there. Here's an example from my practice.

One organisation I worked with were developing scenarios as part of a major change project they had underway. I spent time with senior leaders and managers and interviewed the department heads about their views of the change underway and the future of the organisation. I then worked with a smaller team to build the scenario outlines, fleshed them out and presented them with some supporting material. I was asked to help take them out to the university community which I did happily.

For the most part the scenarios were received in the spirt in which they were intended – as stories about possible futures for the university. In one faculty however, they were rejected by several people who hit assumption walls – they weren't moving into any left-hand quadrant space. They did not want to see, for example, how in one future scenario professional qualifications might not be obtained by getting a degree from a university. The discussion was unpleasant for me and others in the room, eventually stopped by the leader of the project with whom I was working. This resistance had less to do with their acceptance of the need for change and more to do with rejecting new information because it didn't match their worldviews.

During the broader process of presenting the scenarios to staff however, it was clear that most had accepted the need for change, and they were ready. The senior leaders had put a lot of effort into bringing the staff with them on the change journey and at least surfacing some long-held assumptions about the future. As a result, there was energy to change, and while people may have been apprehensive, they were willing to accept that change was inevitable and to make the best of it.

I went back to the organisation about six months later to run a couple of workshops at their senior leaders' conference. In the interim, the change program had been delayed for a number of valid reasons, but the mistake made was not to communicate in any way the reasons for the delay to staff. There were reasons for this too, but the result was that I was standing in a room with very angry and disillusioned people. Their willingness to change had dissipated, leaving the organisation's leaders with a very difficult trust rebuilding task. The organisation was operating solely in the right-hand quadrants again and the lack of trust I could almost feel in the room meant they weren't going into the left-hand quadrant space any time soon.

Here, the initial processes in the right-hand quadrants had tapped into the left-hand quadrants to ensure people understood the need for change and that they had a chance to express their hopes and fears about how the change might play out over time. While seen as necessary, the retreat to the Upper Right Quadrant for the interim six months and the lack of communication about reasons for the delay effectively destroyed the goodwill built up earlier. Staff were no longer 'with' the leaders and felt a disconnect between being part of the change initially and later being isolated from the process.

Finally

Models and frameworks such as the ones discussed in this chapter are only useful if you find them useful and they help you achieve outcomes you want. I provide them here so you can see how I understand the scope of the issues that need to be considered when using foresight in practice and the theory on which I base that understanding. You need this intellectual base to be able to do foresight well.

Bringing Wilber and Slaughter together reminds us that:

- the development of an organisational foresight capacity occurs in a staged way, starting with the individual – it will take time to influence and change habitual ways of thinking across an organisation,
- each level and quadrant must be addressed so that no critical information is 'missed' or ignored in the design of processes, and
- as a result, the four quadrants need to be considered as a whole when designing foresight processes – none of the quadrants are optional.

In strategy terms, ensuring that processes are inclusive of the four quadrants increases the likelihood of that strategy being implemented successfully. By involving people from the beginning of the process as opposed to asking them for feedback when a plan has been drafted, and by designing processes that match the organisation's foresight readiness, a shared view of the preferred future that informs decision making today becomes possible.

4 About Foresight and Strategy

About Foresight

Foresight is first and foremost a state of mind that shapes how you think about the future. That state of mind influences how you design foresight approaches and how you implement them in your organisation. Using foresight calls for ways of thinking and doing that are unlike those required for conventional strategic planning processes.

In the strategy context, foresight is a cognitive, strategic thinking capacity. It is about nurturing the ability to take a forward view to balance historical and present views and to integrate all three views to develop strategy today. Done well, it allows people to identify change that matters early, to assess implications for their organisations and develop adaptive, proactive responses. Using foresight expands perceptions of future options available to an organisation and strengthens the operational context in which strategy is developed. Done less well, it will generate an interesting experience without any deepening of the understanding of the scope of change shaping the organisation's future and resulting strategy will be of the 'cross your fingers and hope' variety.

Why should we take the time to infuse foresight into current strategy approaches? Primarily because the future will not be more of the same or business as usual, tweaked around the edges. Intuitively we recognise this because we know change is all around us. We owe it to ourselves and to those who follow us to understand as best we can the shape of possible futures that might emerge **before** we make strategic decisions today. The aim is to anticipate the future even though the shape of that future is not yet fully formed.

Linking Foresight and Strategy

Strategy is about positioning an organisation for the future, but most information used to inform strategic decision-making today is derived from the past and the present. Using foresight allows organisations to systematically explore their possible futures and begin to understand how external imperatives and challenges might require changing their strategy today. The intention is to craft strategies that are relevant and robust for longer periods of time and that provide a longer-term context for decision making today.

Organisations that carve out time and allocate resources to use foresight will be futures ready and better prepared to deal with any challenges the future might bring them. They will avoid getting the future wrong instead of being focused on getting the future right. The first step in understanding how to use foresight in strategy development is to reframe your understanding of conventional strategic planning.

Reframing Conventional Strategic Planning

Strategic planning has become a routine part of business with an associated set of beliefs and protocols that underpin its day-to-day practice. Its process has been adapted over time but remains basically unchanged. The need to plan has spawned thousands of books, countless software systems and has kept many consultants in work. Yet as Mintzberg (1994) indicates, "planning lacks a clear definition of its own place in organizations" and this conventional approach and its accompanying set of practices has now passed its use by date.

Planning is often defined as an encompassing process that captures all the tasks and processes needed to develop strategy for an organisation's future, including scanning the environment for change, strategic thinking, strategic decision making about future options, documenting and implementing plans and then monitoring outcomes. Strategic planning is not about planning strategically; Mintzberg (1994) reminds us that the term itself is an oxymoron. Strategy is about positioning an organisation for the future while strategic planning is the way we go about documenting action to be taken to implement that strategy today.

Peter & Jarratt (2015) describe two perspectives on planning - prescriptive and descriptive. Conventional planning equates to their prescriptive mode:

> ... strategy development as based on deterministic processes, where the analysis of the organisation, performance, and environment forms a rational, long-term plan. The imposed planning approach embodies a formal process involving the application of traditional analytical tools that assist in defining the organisation and the space in which it competes and tends to locate strategy formation at the top management level.

Using foresight infused strategy development that I describe in this book equates to their emergent and adaptive planning mode that:

> ... views organisations as refining their strategies incrementally as new information indicates changing environments ... strategising involves sense-making around new information, and

de-emphasizing historical constraints ... top management stimulating ideas and structuring the emerging strategic impetuses of the organisational subsystems.

Organisations often respond to rapid change in their external environments by adopting shorter planning cycles where change that's coming that could disrupt an organisation's business model completely is often missed. A longer-term perspective that is structured, formula free, based on strong strategic thinking and that lets new information into the organisation is what is needed now. Taking this longer term approach means treating the future as an asset that can be explored and used on a continuing basis to inform strategy development (Inayatullah, n.d.). Thinking about the future becomes part of strategy and decision making, part of the organisation's culture. Foresight infuses existing strategy processes with the essential futures perspective to a degree that just isn't possible in conventional planning.

Conventional Strategic Planning Challenges

How to explore possible futures to identify a preferred organisational future is for me, one of the least understood components of strategy development. Considering that strategy is being developed to allow the organisation to survive and grow into the future, this is a significant problem with conventional approaches.

Today's issues with planning are not new. It was described by Gerstner (1973) as 'an academic, ill-defined activity with little or no bottom line impact'. Sidorowicz (2000) wrote that 'It may well be that the typical strategic planning exercise now conducted on a regular and formal basis and infused with quantitative data misses the essence of the concept of strategy and what is involved in thinking strategically.' Ashkenas (2013) called defined strategic planning as 'either an over-explained budget or just bad amateur theatre – lots of costumes in the form of analysis, charts and presentations but with very little meaningful substance that can be translated into action'. Yet conventional approaches remain the norm in most organisations. My major issues with conventional strategic planning are described in this section.

The Danger of Seeking Certainty

Conventional approaches to planning seek certainty rather than embracing the uncertainty that characterises the future. Organisational planning departments produce realms of data and charts that lull us into believing that certainty is possible. We humans are programmed for certainty but it infers absolutes, that the right answer is possible. When we believe in the one right way, our cognitive biases kick in when we find that disconfirming evidence that threatens to undermine what we believe to be true:

> *Traditional strategic planning processes as having "choked initiative and favoured incremental over substantive change. They have emphasized analytics and extrapolation rather than creativity and invention ... They have lulled us into complacency with their comforting illusion of certainty in what is in reality a hopelessly uncertain world* (Liedtka 1998).

As a result, we follow a planning formula, we don't seek out alternative futures and we continue to expect that the future will be more of today, tweaked around the edges. This is the official future, the business as usual future, the unchallenged future. Believing in this future means reaction and crisis management are your only choice when change arrives unannounced to you. There is no chance to prepare and you are probably heard to say: 'we didn't see that coming' or 'that was a surprise' and 'what will we do now?'

Inflexibility

If you work in an organisation you probably had the experience of reading a new plan and drafting a set of strategic responses for your area, often retrofitting what you are already doing to align with the plan's goals. Then you put the plan on the shelf and look at it again 12 months later when you have to update it. Worse, when you look at it in 12 months you find the external environment has changed so much that the plan is meaningless and your reporting becomes a compliance exercise.

Change in the external environment during a fixed term plan's timeframe can invalidate some or all of the strategy and the time, money and energy invested in its development will have been wasted. Mid- term reviews of strategic plans are often undertaken and with conventional plans, this is essential to ensure the preferred future described in the plan is still relevant. Foresight infused strategy processes don't lock an organisation in to a fixed set of goals for the duration of the plan, but rather assume goals will need to adapt when - not if - the external environment changes. The focus is on the strategic thinking that informs decision making, rather than making the plan the centre of activity and the only outcome of the planning process.

A Bias Towards Quantitative Data

The bias we have towards certainty and data means that we often ignore and downplay the value of imagination as a valid method for thinking about the future. There are no crystal balls that work so all we have to explore the future is our imaginations – our ideas, hopes, fears, beliefs and images about how the future might evolve. Quantitative data provides but one part of the story and while it is an important source of information when developing strategy, it's not the only one.

Not Involving Staff

While organisations are realising that staff need to be consulted in more authentic ways, strategy development is still regarded as an activity that belongs primarily in the senior management domain. For me, that infers that the belief that only when you have reached senior management status can you think strategically is strong - and we all know that this just isn't true.

Using foresight takes strategy development beyond the realm of senior managers to the rest of the organisation and moves it beyond decisions made by those senior managers and feedback from staff on a fait accompli strategic plan. Instead of strategic thinking being quarantined to specific roles, strategy development becomes an open process accessible by people in the organisation. Value is placed on seeking multiple inputs into strategic thinking and challenging rather than reinforcing deeply held assumptions about how the organisational future might take shape. This is what is called participatory foresight (Borch, Dingli & Jorgensen, 2013).

Everyone in an organisation can think strategically if given the opportunity and the information about change that was quarantined previously to certain parts of the organisation. The key word here is opportunity – not everyone will want to be involved, some will see it as outside their job, some will see it as senior managers trying to give them more work to do and some won't care. There will be a sizeable group however, who will accept the opportunity and commit to being involved. They are the people who can help you expand and strengthen your thinking about possible futures for your organisation.

Managers, leaders and CEOs are generally not paid to admit they are uncertain about anything and they often have a strong emotional investment in the status quo that they helped to build even if they don't recognise it. The result? They don't let new and disconfirming information into the organisation, they create plans that pay lip service to the future and then almost insult staff when they ask for their comments on a plan when it's too late to change it. This is not, as Liedtka (2011, p. 29) points out, to suggest that the conventional process for developing strategy isn't approached seriously and with good intentions, but it fails when it comes to execution:

The idea that strategy exists within the realm of thought is pervasive ... It urges strategic planning processes that utilize conscious forethought, commit aspirations and plans to paper, generally include a strong quantitative component, stress effective communication and carefully measure and monitor outcomes. In short, it makes a great deal of sense ... The problem managers face is that this approach does not appear to be working very well: the gap between strategic rhetoric and strategic action remains frustrating.

It is increasingly obvious that conventional planning based on certainties and focused on the executive suite no longer delivers meaningful and relevant outcomes. Why? Because even if you have involved staff in your strategy development process, conventional approaches produce rational strategy that is knowable on an intellectual basis, what Liedtka calls 'strategy as thought'. People can know what the strategy is but Liedtka's argument (that made me almost jump for joy when I read the paper) is that strategy must be 'felt' for it be effective. Strategy as felt is based on the idea that each of us has a worldview that helps us interpret reality as we seek for 'satisfying authenticity', "the intersection of the *objectively real* and the *desirable*" (Liedtka 2011, p.30). This means helping people to move from knowing about strategy to caring about it:

... an even more fundamental and seemingly obvious cause may underlie the longstanding failure to align word with deed:

nobody really cares about these strategies. Leaders must move beyond incorporating solid strategic thinking and effective communication in order to succeed: strategies must be felt as personally meaningful and compelling by the members of the organization who must adopt new behaviours in order to execute them.

The aim with foresight infused strategy is to reach the position where staff can see themselves in the preferred future that is developed – a preferred future that they want to help achieve. They will only feel this way if they have been involved in the development process. To avoid plans being ignored we must move strategy from being written down to strategy as experienced, strategy as felt. That means a focus not only on goals but also desires, since it is desire that is the motivator for people to change what they do and how they do it. New strategic processes focused on people are needed:

To summarize, strategy as thought emphasizes the effective communication of mission statements and plans; it utilizes conscious forethought to create these, and outcome metrics to monitor their implementation. Strategy as experienced, on the other hand, relies more heavily on dialogue-based strategic conversation as its foundation, with significant use of stories and metaphors, developed iteratively in an experimental approach. Rather than relying on outcome metrics as a control device, it finds sustainability in the energy produced by the process itself (Liedtka, 2011, p. 31).

How you bring people into strategy development will depend on how your organisation operates, and its current culture will be a major determinant of how you design these processes. I've spent a bit of time on this section on involving people because strategy developed with open input, aiming for strategy as experienced **will** be stronger than if strategy is viewed as something to be accepted intellectually and without question. Remember that strategy without people is strategy without a future.

The Solution: From Strategic Planning to Foresight Infused Strategy

Conventional strategic planning lives in what Slaughter (2004) calls the pragmatic foresight realm. This is where we work within the existing planning paradigm, adapting it, making it better, but not challenging its underpinning assumptions. To move beyond strategic planning to foresight infused strategy development, we need to move into the **progressive** foresight realm, where the current planning paradigm is challenged. Continuous change and uncertainty forces reinterpretations of our expectations about how we do business to meet the challenges of the future. It is in this space that new ways of thinking about the future emerge.

The need to move from conventional planning and its formulaic and top down approach is not unrecognised:

> ...we need to break free of this obsession with planning. Strategy is not planning — it is the making of an integrated set of choices that collectively position the firm in its industry so as to create sustainable advantage relative to competition and deliver superior financial returns. (Martin 2013)

> Strategy is less a route map of how we are to navigate the future (since we do not know the whole map) but more an assessment of an institution's capacity to be agile and flexible in the face of emergent and unpredictable change. (Wooldridge 2010)

Foresight infused strategy development does not discount the need for a plan. Strategic planning is instead viewed as the last step in strategy development rather than the driver of the process. This move to a new way of developing strategy where everyone in the organisation can be involved, where collaborative processes are central, where those processes are beyond formulaic and designed for the needs of each organisation will be inevitable as conventional approaches continue to fail in the execution stage. This approach focuses not on a formulaic set of outcomes – Vision, Mission, Goals, Objectives, Action, KPIS – but around a set of core questions (Table 2). It builds on the past and the present to be able to face to the future. It moves beyond language like empowerment and alignment to a new set of words like flow, ecosystem and collaboration. It moves strategy out of the senior management realm to everyone in the organisation.

Table 2: Core Foresight Questions

Strategy Stage	Question(s)
Opening Minds	Are we ready to face the future?
Acknowledging the Past and the Present	How did we get here? What do we do today?
Facing the Future	What change is shaping our organisation's future? What change matters most for our organisation?
Exploring the Future	What are our possible futures? What would we do in each of those possible futures?
Connecting the Future and the Present	What makes strategic sense given our capacities and resources today, both real and potential? Are we considering the needs of future generations in our decisions?
Crafting Strategic Intent	What will we do now?
Taking Action	How will we do that today?

The questions appear simple but getting to the answers is not. The challenge is to answer them more deeply than conventional approaches allow; you need time to think about them before answering. To answer them means surfacing the assumptions and cognitive biases that have constrained how you may have responded to change in the past. To answer them with an eye to the future as well as the past and the present. To answer them in collaboration with everyone in your organisation. To explore all the changes shaping the future and your organisation's possible futures before you make decisions and take action. To be open to see beyond today's ways of operating.

Using Foresight for Strategy

If we are to move our focus away from conventional strategic planning to foresight infused strategy development, the critical distinction that must be made is between strategic planning and strategic thinking. Successful strategy needs as much emphasis placed on strategic thinking as is now placed on strategic planning. As Wilson (1997) writes, "there is little to be gained from developing a plan per se. There is everything to be gained from the thinking that lies behind the plan – and the action that follows it."

Mintzberg (1994) writes that **strategic planning** is about taking an articulated goal and turning it into formal, documented action steps that can be implemented to achieve agreed results. This sort of activity requires thinking that is analytical, logical, pragmatic and deductive to make sure that actions are implemented, monitored and reported. By contrast, Mintzberg (1994) suggests that **strategic thinking** is about synthesis. Liedtka (1998) indicates that this thinking is intuitive, experimental and necessarily disruptive, and aims to explore areas beyond logical thinking, in order to develop a vision of an organisation's future. Because information about potential futures is always incomplete, the thinking required for success needs to be 'synthetical' and inductive, rather than analytical and deductive. Table 3 summarises the differences between the purpose and thought processes of strategic thinking and strategic planning.

Table 3: Purpose and Thought Processes of Strategic Thinking and Strategic Planning (Heracleous & Jacobs 2008)

Activity	Purpose	Thought Process
Strategic Thinking	Discover novel, imaginative strategies that can re-write the rules of the competitive game; and to envision potential futures; significantly different from the present.	Synthetic Divergent Creative Beyond linear
Strategic Planning	Operationalise strategies developed through strategic thinking, and to support the strategic thinking process.	Analytical Convergent Conventional Pragmatic

There are also differences between how strategic thinking and strategic planning position the future, the strategy process and the outcomes. Table 4 summarises these differences in approach.

Table 4: The Difference between Strategic Thinking and Strategic Planning (Adapted from Liedtka, 1998)

Strategic Thinking	Strategic Planning
Only the shape of the future can be predicted	The future is predictable and specifiable in detail
Relies on self-reference – a sense of strategic intent and purpose embedded in the minds of people that guide their choices	Asserts control through measurement
Requires that people have an understanding of the larger system	Assumes that individuals need only to know his or her own role well
Sees strategy and change as inescapably linked and assumes that finding new strategic options and implementing them successfully is harder and more important than evaluating them	Assumes that the challenge of setting strategic direction is primarily analytic
Sees the planning process itself as a critical value-adding element	Focus on the creation of the plan as the ultimate object

Leidtka makes the point that while strategic thinking has been valued for mangers and leaders for many years, "what is new is the belief that organizational members below the level of senior executive now need to possess the ability to thinking strategically. It is the diffusion of strategic thinking capabilities throughout the organization that presents the challenge to business as usual."

When we were working at Swinburne, Joseph Voros and I saw strategic thinking at the core of foresight work:

> *Foresight in an organisational context is best conceived and positioned as an aspect of strategic thinking, which is meant to open up an expanded range of perceptions of the strategic options available, so that strategy making is potential wiser. Strategic thinking is concerned with exploration, often based on limited and patchy information and options, not the steps needed for implementation of actions, which is the realm of strategic planning.* (Conway & Voros 2002)

In summary, strategic thinking is first a divergent process, seeking a wide and diverse range of perspectives about strategic issues and change shaping those issues. Nothing is ignored initially, much like a brainstorming process. It also looks for emergence by challenging assumptions to identify factors and trends not previously seen or missed because of cognitive biases. Convergence via the planning process uses the output from strategic thinking to identify action that can be taken today.

The Generic Foresight Process Framework

Figure 5 shows the Generic Foresight Process Framework that indicates clearly that there is a structured and integrated process for using foresight in strategy development. Using foresight is not an add-on or an optional extra – it needs to infuse strategy development from the very beginning of the process.

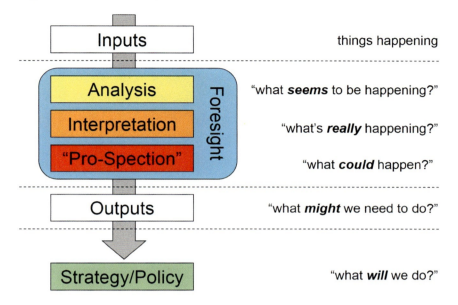

Figure 5: Generic Foresight Process (Copyright Joseph Voros 2000)

The Generic Foresight Process proceeds broadly as follows. You gather **inputs** (information about changes in the external environment you are seeing) by using environmental scanning (Chapter 7). The blue foresight box and its three steps are the home of strategic thinking (Chapter 8), where you expand and deepen your understanding of change shaping your organisation's future and implications for action today. Chapter 6 provides more information on the methods you can use at each point of this process.

The **Analysis** step asks what seems to be happening out there that is relevant for us? This step contextualises the information to suit the organisation. The **Interpretation** step asks what do those things mean for us and in what ways are they important? What is the deeper structure here? What's significant and what's not? What insights emerge? Whose voice isn't being heard? The **Prospection** step, the step most organisations miss, asks what are the alternative future outcomes for our organisation that offer us the best chance of success – what might happen? These three steps taken together are the domain of strategic thinking.

Finally, you produce tangible outputs, the product of a foresight exercise that informs decision making about strategic options. You will also produce intangible outputs in the form of thinking shifts, especially those insights generated during Interpretation work. Joseph Voros (2003) wrote that these thinking shifts are "undoubtedly the more important form of output because of the way it alters the very mechanism of strategy development itself, namely the perceptions of the mind(s) involved in strategizing".

Conventional planning approaches usually take you from Inputs to Analysis/Interpretation to Decision Making skipping the Prospection step. If this is how your organisation develops strategy - and most still do - you are creating strategy that has a context based on what you know about the past and the present, rather than a future context where possible outcomes of change over time has been explored using prospective tools. With no understanding of possible, plausible and probable futures and how they might evolve, it is assumed that tomorrow will be business as usual.

Other Foresight Frameworks

There are other ways of describing how to use foresight in practice. Table 5 provides a summary of six alternative frameworks – and there are many others.

Table 5: Some Foresight Frameworks

Framework	Process Steps
Horton (1999) *A successful foresight process*	Inputs (collection, collation and summarizing) Foresight (translation and interpretation) Outputs and Action (assimilation and commitment)
Inayatullah (2013) *Six pillars: futures thinking for transforming*	Mapping Anticipating Timing Deepening Creating Transforming
Bishop & Hines (2007) *Thinking about the Future: Guidelines for Strategic Foresight*	Framing Scanning Forecasting Visioning Planning Action
Schultz (2006) *Key activities of integrated foresight*	Identify and Monitor change Assess and Critique Impacts Imagine Alternative Outcomes Envision Preferred Futures Plan and Implement Change
Keenan (2007) *Five mental acts (stages) for Foresight*	Understanding Synthesising and models of the future Analysis and selection Transformation Action
Farrington, Henson & Crews *(2012)* *Research Foresights: The Use of Strategic Foresight Methods for Ideation and Portfolio Management*	Discovery Extrapolation Integration Planning

No matter what terms are used and how many discussions are held about the 'right' or 'appropriate' terms to use, remember that foresight is at its core about exploring change to deepen insights about possible futures to inform strategic decision making today. At its most basic when we ask people to use foresight we are asking them to:

- expand their perceptual horizons to **look more broadly** to see what's changing (scanning),
- **think** more deeply about the implications of that change, explore how it might evolve over time, and identify a wider range of possible strategic responses and actions (strategic thinking), and then
- **decide** on what to do today and take action (planning).

Making Strategy

When it comes to using foresight in strategy development, I've adapted these frameworks to create a four stage process. For me, the development of effective, meaningful and futures ready strategy by using foresight involves these four separate, distinct and interdependent stages as shown in Figure 6: environmental scanning, strategic thinking, strategic decision making and strategic planning.

Environmental scanning seeks information about change to provide input into the other stages. The quality of that input is directly related to the quality of outputs, so doing scanning well is a critical step in the foresight process. Chapter 7 provides more information on doing scanning.

Strategic thinking uses processes to help you develop a deeper understanding of change to inform the creation of a range of alternative futures for your organisation, and to use that knowledge to expand your thinking about your potential strategic options today. For me this space is the core foresight domain where new ways of thinking about the future emerge. Chapter 8 provides more information on strategic thinking.

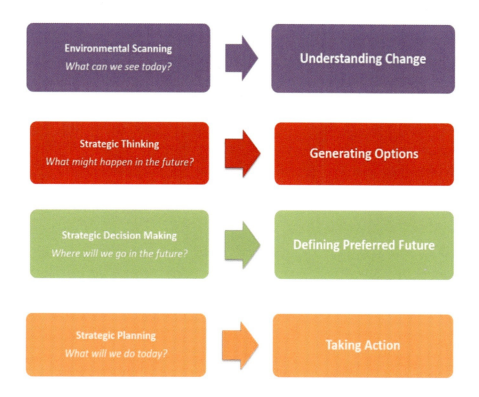

Figure 6: Four Level Strategy Development Process

Strategic thinking uses processes to help you develop a deeper understanding of change to inform the creation of a range of alternative futures for your organisation, and to use that knowledge to expand your thinking about your potential strategic options today. For me this space is the core foresight domain where new ways of thinking about the future emerge. Chapter 8 provides more information on strategic thinking.

Deciding **on a preferred future** will always be the realm of the Board or CEO or whatever groups governs your organisation. They make the decision about strategic direction, ideally only after a defined and organisation wide open strategic thinking process has informed that decision.

Strategic planning is focused on documenting action, measures and accountability and ensuring that action is completed. I wrote earlier about the notion of a plan being viewed as more fluid to allow actions to be adapted as the external environment changes could mean that in some contexts, a plan in the conventional sense may not be needed. New language may also be needed, moving away from terms such as vision, mission, goals and KPIs to 'our future', 'how we will get there' and 'how will we know when we have arrived'.

The focus is therefore not on producing a glossy, expensive publication which becomes an artifact no one uses. Instead, a plan becomes a reference point for decision making, ensuring people share a common understanding of their preferred future and how they can contribute to reaching it, both individually and collectively.

5 Using Foresight: Getting Started

Before going 'live' in an organisation with foresight processes, there are some preliminary steps that you should take to ensure you have a firm foundation for your work. In Wilber's four quadrant model terms (see Chapter 3), you will need to understand:

- **Upper Left Quadrant**: your positioning in the organisation, what you personally hope to get out of using foresight approaches in your organisation, and your worldview because that is how you interpret what goes on in your organisation,
- **Upper Right Quadrant**: how to design and adapt organisational processes to integrate foresight approaches that have people and collaboration at the core,
- **Lower Right Quadrant**: what information about change will need to be identified and analysed to inform strategic thinking in your organisation and how you will do that, and
- **Lower Left Quadrant**: how organisational culture and politics might affect your implementation plan; you will need to identify who should be involved if you are to be successful and understand clearly what will and won't work in your organisation at the present time.

Remember that you will develop 'deeper' and more effective processes if you develop depth in your own critical thinking and self reflection skills. It should be clear by now that the ability to challenge the apparently obvious assumptions about change shaping the future of your organisation is a fundamental foresight competency.

Your Positioning: 10 Questions

Hines (2003) asks 10 questions every organisational futurist needs to be able to answer. It should be compulsory reading for anyone wanting to use foresight work in organisations. Here's my summary of the 10 questions.

1   How are you going to spend your time?

Are you going to focus on process, content, or transformation (changing minds)? My view is that you should focus on 90% process and 10% content to begin with, getting the process right while making sure your content is credible. The reality is that you might never reach the transformation stage at the organisation level. Ultimately, using foresight is about changing the way we think about the future, and transformation at both an individual and organisational level will not only be challenging but will take some time.

2   What is your positioning?

This question is about understanding your position in the organisation. Hines describes a spectrum ranging from an inside focus – you work within the organisation, to planners, to 'insider-outsiders' and finally at the outside focus, you have a public voice for your organisation. Somewhere down towards the insider end of the spectrum is the option of working in 'stealth mode' which is something that needs to be considered at times when there are significant obstacles to developing a foresight program.

3   What is your leadership style?

Hines writes that every futurist has to be a leader of some kind and provides another spectrum from leader-oriented to participant-oriented and from coercive to democratic styles. I think that foresight leadership builds over time – until you are confident in your understanding of foresight work, I would not try and lead from the front – but that's where you must aim to be eventually!

4   What is your framework?

There are three broad areas in which futurists work in organisations: (i) the strategic, (ii) the creative, and (iii) the educational. The first has to do with informing organisational strategy and decision making, the second with generating new ideas, and the third with a general information role about the future. Your foresight work will need to be clear about which of these areas it will address.

5   Who is your audience?

Hines describes four organisational types: (i) true believers who will follow you anywhere (ii) bridge builders, who understand the organisation and its politics (iii) fence-sitters, who are prepared to support you as long as there is something in it for them and (iv) laggards, who will never support you. Aim your futures message at the bridge builders, who will know how to help you get foresight accepted or at least tolerated in the organisation.

6   Who is in your network?

As with most organisational work, it is important to build both internal and external networks. This is particularly true with foresight work, and connecting with the foresight community is worth the effort. The major futures/foresight associations are the World Futures Society, the World Future Studies Federation, and the Association of Professional Futurists.

7 What is in your toolkit?

This is about methods (Chapter 6). Hines recommends you have a relatively broad toolkit of methods, so that you are able to work in different contexts with different groups of people. Start with one or two methods and build your expertise in these first, and then work to introduce a broader range of approaches.

8 What is your guiding orientation?

At what level of depth do you want to work? In foresight work, you can work at the 'pop' level, which is a mostly superficial, techno-wow type approach, which gets people thinking about the future but in a superficial way. Deeper is the problem-oriented approach which is the focus of most organisational work, and emphasises decision making and options in the near term future. Yet deeper is critical futures, the realm of meaning and paradigms and epistemological futures work where the foundations of social order are explored – these need to be used with caution and delayed until the organisation is ready for them.

9 What are your purposes?

Are you going to focus on being more creative, being able to deal with change better, being more futures focused, or thinking more deeply and systemically? You need to decide what you are trying to do before you do it. This is a personal purpose for using foresight rather than organisational purpose.

10   What are your intended uses?

Are your desired outcomes to do with improving the quality of information to inform strategic decision making, looking for issues that need to be addressed, focusing on problem solving or simply increasing the level of knowledge about foresight work in your organisation?

Start-Up

Once you have done your own personal audit using Hines' 10 questions, you are ready to consider how best to set up your foresight function. Not every organisation will have the resources to set up an in-house foresight unit even with top level commitment. Slaughter (1999, pp.290–291) suggests that there are four ways to start using foresight in organisations:

- upgrade an existing capacity,
- create a new capacity, and
- buy in external expertise, or
- a combination of the above.

Upgrading an existing capacity was how my foresight work began, where my role in planning was expanded to include using foresight. **Creating a new capacity** is probably the most expensive option, but allows you to tailor the structure and processes to your needs. It also allows you to ensure that people brought in and transferred from within have the right capacities and levels of knowledge and expertise.

Buying in external expertise can be useful, and there are many foresight consultants who would be able to work with you to establish the function. In this case, you need to ensure that knowledge transfer is part of the agreement so that you are not reliant on consultants on a continuing basis.

Combining all three to create a fourth approach may well be what happens in practice, but that decision will depend on your funding and your rationale for wanting to use foresight.

Prerequisites for Successful Foresight Practice

There are some essential prerequisites to using foresight in your organisation. In this section, I am assuming you are working in a foresight role in an organisation.

Organisational Commitment

Before starting to use foresight, overt recognition and acceptance of the value of systematically considering the future as part of strategy development is essential. Without this organisational commitment you won't be able to infuse foresight into existing strategy processes and time and resources are unlikely to be allocated to using foresight. That means acceptance of foresight will always be dependent on individual champions rather than being embedded into organisational strategy processes.

You first job is to convince leaders of the value of foresight. How do you do that? That depends on the individual – some just won't be interested while others will be willing to give it a go. You will be able to identify genuine interest pretty quickly and it may help to position an exercise as a pilot to test foresight readiness rather than propose a permanent addition to your strategy development from the beginning.

Spend time with the people who are the decision makers to build their understanding of foresight, its value and how they think it should be introduced. Coalitions are important when you are attempting to introduce a new process that will inevitably disrupt existing planning and strategy processes. This is Hines' point about knowing your audiences.

Clarity around Purpose

Know why you are using foresight. What is your purpose? How will you integrate foresight activity into your existing processes and what you will do with the outcomes? If you don't do this, you will end up with a process that isn't connected to your strategy development or that produces outcomes no one uses. Spend some time here to get it right.

An Agreed Time Frame

In Chapter 3, I talked about the need to use a minimum of a 10-year time frame to help people move their thinking beyond today, to help them let go of unhelpful assumptions underpinning their views of the future. Ten years is usually enough to demonstrate that while some things stay the same, many more will change in radical ways. At the same time, you know your organisation and you want using foresight to be accepted as a permanent addition to your strategy development; you will know how far out to go. It's my experience that while people will think 10 years is too far out, they will engage when you remind them that the process is about the new, what's coming over the horizon, not about taking today into the future.

Clear Ground Rules and Expectations

This was something we did not do well at Swinburne. There were mixed understandings about what we were trying to do and confusion about how the foresight work linked with our planning system. Infusing foresight into existing strategy processes will be incremental in most cases, and it will challenge conventional wisdom about how to plan. To avoid confusion, you need to be very clear about:

- the rationale for using foresight,
- the role of foresight work and unit, and who will be involved and why,

- what resources are being expended to fund the set-up costs of the work,
- how foresight work will be communicated to the organisation and beyond,
- what methods will be used and why,
- how the output will be used and how it will link to existing processes, and
- how performance and results will be evaluated.

Well Trained People

Train the people who will be leading your foresight processes. This may be a formal course or a professional development program or even a mentoring arrangement where you get support with design/implementation when you need it. Foresight is not planning, and people involved in the shift need to understand the difference and be well grounded in foresight principles and concepts.

What's next?

You have organisational commitment, you know why you are using foresight, what you will do with the outcomes and who will be involved. What do you do now?

Do an Internal Foresight Audit

There are two components to an internal foresight audit. This first addresses Wilber's left-hand quadrants where people are engaged directly to understand how they view the future now. Interview senior managers, survey staff, hold workshops, whatever works in your context. Ask questions like:

- What are we assuming about the future in our current strategy?
- What are the questions about the future for which we have no answers?
- What changes are coming over the horizon that are likely to have the most significant impact on our organisation?
- What is a good future for our organisation?
- What is the most critical decision we have to make in the next couple of years?

These types of questions will help you identify both unquestioned assumptions about the future, the types of change likely to shape your organisation's future evolution and operations and the nature of strategic issues that are occupying minds. It will probably also give you some idea about the unwritten rules about how your organisation operates and its organisational culture. This information will help you design a foresight approach that works in your context as well as highlighting the strategic issues that can be explored by using foresight.

The second component addresses Wilber's right hand quadrants and is about identifying what sort of foresight information already exists in the organisation. It is likely that there are already overt and tacit processes in the organisation that collect information about the external environment, so an audit of this information and ways in which it is used is often useful to identify both strengths and gaps in that information. You also need to consider which staff may have knowledge about change that will be useful in your foresight work, and how those staff might contribute to your processes.

Identify People Who Are Suited to Foresight Work

Using internal capacity is one way to establish a foresight function but with this approach care needs to be taken when you assess the capabilities and expertise of existing staff. Not everyone is suited to this sort of work, since it does challenge long held ways of organisational operating and thinking on both an individual and collective level. You can use my characteristics of foresighters to help you find people who are open to the future.

- I am open to new ideas, including to what others might call weird and strange. I sometimes think outrageously.
- I am curious. I want to know why it is so. I'm a good observer.
- I think outside the box. I understand my industry but I'm interested in global change as well.
- I try to think in systems, to understand the whole, the big picture and not get trapped in my silo.
- I am aware of my own worldview and understand where my blind spots are.
- I am usually optimistic about the future.
- I challenge assumptions about the future, mine and others.
- I value diversity. I understand the perspectives are neither right nor wrong but just are.
- I am resilient. I understand that the value of foresight to better understand the future may sometimes be difficult to communicate and that resistance is to be expected.
- I trust and value my expertise and knowledge to be able to identify observations relevant and important to my organisation's future.

The most critical characteristic in my experience is resilience. Because foresight approaches challenge the value of conventional and familiar strategic planning and the beliefs people have about the future, there will be resistance. Resilience is important to allow you to keep going with foresight and to manage your own emotions and reactions in the face of often strong resistance from people who don't like their views being challenged.

Many of these characteristics relate to your ability to be self-reflexive, consciously reflecting on how your values, beliefs and ways of operating shape how the future is perceived in your organisation. It's a form of meta-reflection, a critique of yourself and how and why you are operating and thinking as you are, the circumstances and relationships you are dealing with, and where you might need to change what you do and how you do it to achieve different outcomes. It's an ability to put yourself in the situation and understand how you influence what is going on and maintain structures and ways of thinking that may be counterproductive. To be able to engage with the future openly, this ability to critique yourself is essential.

Use Wilber to Frame your Foresight Approach

Designing how you will introduce foresight and link it to existing strategic planning practices can be one of the most exciting stages in foresight work. Here you are putting into action all the planning and thinking you have been doing. One way is to use Wilber's four quadrant framework shown in Figure 7. Some indicative methods to use in each quadrant are provided in this figure; you can find out more about the methods in Chapter 6.

Each quadrant lends itself to particular methods or processes. The **Upper Left** quadrant needs engagement with staff directly to obtain their views about the future of an organisation. While the Wilber view of the world suggests that staff views should be sought directly in one-on-one interviews for example, that is often impractical in the real world of organisational strategy. Focus groups and surveys can provide rich data. Involving people in workshops to create alternative futures is more resource intensive but has the advantage of exposing people to foresight methods and thinking and potentially surface their foresight capacities.

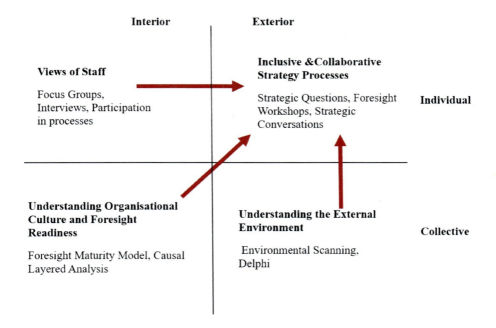

Figure 7: Doing Foresight Work Using Wilber's Four Quadrants

The **Lower Left** quadrant focuses on ensuring that organisational culture is taken into account when you use foresight. This seems logical enough, but unless you ensure that you have processes that allow those organisational 'undiscussables' to be surfaced you may again face implementation issues. Causal Layered Analysis (Inayatullah, 2004) for example, allows a contentious issue to be explored in depth and then to be reframed in a more positive and shared way.

The **Lower Right** quadrant is the world of environmental scanning, SWOT and STEEP, trend analysis and many, many consultancy services. When work here is done well, it provides extraordinary input into foresight work. When it is done poorly foresight work risks failure because of low credibility and/or narrow scope and depth. The need for high quality scanning and information about the external environment is critical.

The **Upper Right** quadrant is where strategy development processes occur – research, workshops, conversations, decisions and documentation. It is a clearly understood realm in terms of conventional planning, again with many consultancy services. The same caveats apply. Processes need to be designed for the organisation and done well to be of any lasting value. The Foresight Maturity Model (Chapter 6) provides a perspective on your organisation's foresight readiness and highlights gaps in your processes.

As already indicated but worth repeating, all four quadrants overlap and depend on each other, and you need to address all four when you use foresight approaches in your organisation. It seems logical to want to ensure you don't spend a lot of time in the right hand quadrants developing a plan only to see if fail because the left hand quadrants haven't been taken into account.

A word about people

Design your foresight approach with people at the core and collaboration in all your activities. Invite people into the process rather than exclude them by virtue of their role in the organisation and get them collaborating on thinking about the future. You are looking for diversity of perspectives, to broaden and open up understanding of change from what is certain to what is possible. Seek out alternative views of the future from within and outside your organisation, from people who support you and people who are your critics. You will be surprised at the quality of thinking that begins to emerge if people are given the opportunity and the information that provides a common starting point to discussions.

Including people in this way does require preparation and time to gather information and run processes not usually included in conventional approaches. Providing opportunities for staff to be involved in strategic thinking processes is a positive sign of an organisation being serious about using foresight approaches. Some ways to facilitate the use of those approaches across an organisation can include:

- seek staff views about the future of the organisation in a structured way which could range from surveys to online conversation/idea spaces and online games,
- provide all staff with opportunities to hear about changes affecting the organisation and provide information about those changes on a continuing basis,
- even better, set up a scanning system that allows staff to share the changes they think are critical to consider,
- schedule regular thinking workshops during the year for people to come together for facilitated strategic conversations about change and the future and identify common themes, and
- involve people in strategy workshops at the level of the organisation most relevant to their roles and expertise – move beyond the conventional off-site, once a year planning workshop to continually seeking input using a range of methods.

These are only a few ideas. You will need to determine what fits your organisation and what will and won't engage people in using foresight – try to move beyond conventional approaches, particularly when there are many digital tools today to help you connect your staff to enable them to share their views.

Run a pilot process - start small

We made the mistake at Swinburne of starting BIG, launching foresight as the next best thing in strategy development. Resistance emerged because of this: people felt it was being imposed on them without any warning and some said they felt like they were being taught about foresight and didn't like it – an important reminder for me that experience is a better way to learn about the value of foresight. We found that when we worked with individuals and departments however, the response was very positive. So start small – particularly if you don't have strong organisation wide commitment from all leaders and managers.

Environmental scanning is a good place to start. It can be opened up to people in the organisation quickly and is non-threatening because it's focused on understanding change. No one should argue about the value of doing that. Use the scanning output as the input into a thinking workshop or events across the organisation, where the idea is to have strategic conversations that demonstrate the value of opening up minds to the future and exploring beyond the linear, projected future. Be flexible and adaptive. Look for ways to generate that small ripple that turns into a foresight tsunami. Focus where you are making impact and take people with you on a foresight learning journey.

Communicate and Communicate Often

Using foresight should be a productive exercise to demonstrate value. You need to let people know what is happening, invite participation, share output and outcomes, and let them be involved in review and decision making (for example, something as simple as rating the importance of scanning outcomes). The aim is for information about change to permeate your organisation to increase awareness of how that change is shaping your organisation's future – and how that future will be different compared to today. Importantly, remember that in the beginning you will probably know more about foresight than the people with whom you are communicating. Start from their position, their level of knowledge about foresight, not yours.

Finally

Taking the time to develop the foundations for your foresight work by following the steps in this chapter may seem like a lot of work. It probably is, but starting a foresight exercise without having done this work is quite risky in two ways.

First, people involved in foresight processes need to be able to understand the value of foresight and see that it can provide new ways of thinking about the organisation's future and what that means for them in their work. If you haven't designed those processes around them in ways that will demonstrate this value, you risk losing their support very early. Second, I am assuming that if you are reading the book you are likely to want to embed foresight into your organisation's strategy processes. If you can't show clearly how using foresight will strengthen strategic thinking capacity to produce more robust strategy that improves decision making today, that will never happen. This chapter was designed to help you mitigate those risks and provide the best foundation possible for your foresight work.

6   Using Foresight: Methods Overview

I'm not going to pretend that this chapter will give you a comprehensive discussion of every method that you could use in your foresight program. Choosing foresight methods depends on your purpose, your organisation's foresight readiness and your desired outcomes. There is no preferred list of methods applicable to every situation.

Using the Generic Foresight Process Framework (Chapter 4), there are four types of methods corresponding to each foresight stage:

- **input** methods - what is happening out there?
- **analytic** methods – what patterns are emerging?
- **interpretive** methods – but, what's really happening? and
- **prospective** methods – now, what might happen?

Using one method on its own without a foresight framework in place may be useful in the short term. For example, many organisations do environmental scanning but the focus of the scanning is often mainstream sources rather than the periphery where emerging signals of change emerge. Likewise, I know many people who have picked up a book on scenario thinking, followed the steps, and ran what they consider a successful process. Using these methods in isolation will probably be interesting and somewhat challenging, but will contribute little to shift assumptions about how possible futures might emerge. Both the choice of method and the way it is applied must be considered carefully if meaningful outcomes are to be achieved.

Most conventional approaches will use input and analytic methods and perhaps some form of interpretive method. Most omit the prospective stage where alternative futures are explored. Only if each of these four types of methods are employed can we begin to say that we have considered the future in strategy development. As already indicated, it is this combination of input, analysis, interpretation and prospection methods that enables organisations to craft futures ready strategy.

When to Use a Method

The methods I've included in this chapter are the ones I use most often as well as the ones I am learning to be able to add to my toolbox. Foresight practitioners usually have a toolbox of methods from which they draw, depending on the context in which they are working, the purpose of the particular activity being undertaken and the desired outcomes. Those toolboxes also reflect the worldview of the practitioner, what they prefer using, what they think will get the 'best' outcomes. If you are choosing methods to use in your organisation, you must be alert to your own preferences and biases and ensure the method you select is the most appropriate for the organisation, not the one you prefer or feel more comfortable using. For example, organisations just starting to use foresight will probably need different methods compared to an organisations that has used foresight for some time. Choosing a method with you aren't familiar may mean getting someone from outside your organisation to help, but this is preferable to using the wrong method or using a method badly.

Foresight Maturity Model

The choice of method depends on a number of factors such as experience in using the method and resources available. For me, the most important factor is the readiness of an organisation to use foresight tools to inform strategic thinking. The Foresight Maturity Model (Grim 2009) is a way 'to establish a baseline and plan for developing powerful internal foresight capacities' by measuring your organisation's foresight status in relation to a set of statements describing good foresight work. The model assesses a number of practices across several areas of activity and uses five outcome levels:

- **Ad hoc** – the organisation is not or only marginally aware of processes,
- **Aware** – the organisation is aware that there are best practices* in the field and is learning,
- **Capable** – the organisation has reached a level where it has a consistent approach for a practice across the organisation,
- **Mature** – the organisation has developed expertise and advanced processes, and
- **World-Class** – the organisation is considered a leader in this area, often developing new methods

*Bear in mind what I said about best practice in Chapter 1. The FMM describes good foresight work as it is understood today. It is a useful starting point because it gives you an overview of the factors involved in developing an organisational foresight capacity. Use the results only as a guide to inform your design of your foresight work – they are a good starting point.

Assessing your organisation using the FMM will give you an idea about which method is most appropriate at any given time. For example, if an organisation is at ad hoc stage across a range of areas, easily understood methods would need to be used such as environmental scanning or strategic thinking. A mature organisation could use more complex methods such as Causal Layered Analysis. At the risk of repeating myself, you will have an idea about your organisation's foresight readiness. Use the information you get from the FMM and your own research to inform your decision making about choice of methods.

Foresight Diamond

Developed by Rafael Popper (2013) the Foresight Diamond (Figure 8) includes a wide range of possible methods, categorised in four ways:

- **Creativity based methods**: require original and imaginative thinking, based largely on expertise and intuition,
- **Expertise based methods**: based on the skill and knowledge of experts in a particular subject area,
- **Interaction based methods**: use collaborative expertise and allows participation by a wide range of people, and
- **Evidence based methods**: largely quantitative in nature, seek explanation based on documented evidence and data.

The Foresight Diamond can also be used to select methods across the four types. Remember that if your organisation is data driven in its decision making, it may not favour creative methods just yet. Using methods from more than one category is also useful but again, choice depends upon your organisation's context and foresight maturity today.

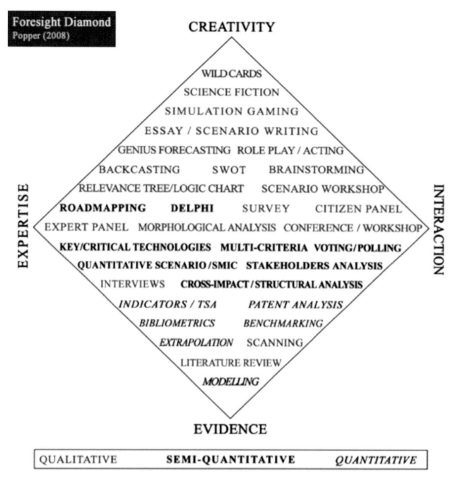

Figure 8: Foresight Diamond (from Popper 2008)

Input Methods

Input methods focus on the collection of high quality information about change in the external environment likely to affect your organisation's future. The question being asked here is 'what's going on out there?' or 'what's happening?' The aim is to identify changes in the external environment that are important and relevant for your organisation.

Delphi

Delphi is a structured group communication process for gathering expert opinion about a complex problem for which there is incomplete knowledge. Typically, this is a long term problem or issue with participant judgements therefore made in the face of uncertainty. Since the long term future of any issue is inherently uncertain, Delphi is an appropriate method for obtaining expert opinion and their views about how the future might evolve for a given context (For-Learn, 2006).

Views about the issue are obtained over a number of rounds. The usual aim is to generate consensus by the time the final round is completed. Delphi is useful where a high degree of source credibility is required and where uncertainty of outcomes is assumed. The key question to ask here, as with all methods, is what images of the future are generated in this output (to allow explorations of possible strategic options)? And, whose voice is not being heard in this process (to ensure inclusivity and diversity)?

Delphi takes time and resources. It has traditionally been a manual exercise but it's moving online. One example is the Millennium Project site which runs real time Delphi processes that are generally open to the public. I would use Delphi in an organisation just starting out with foresight, or as a follow up to environmental scanning to identify what change people inside and outside your organisation think matters most for you.

Environmental Scanning

Every organisation should have a formal, organisation wide scanning system. Environmental scanning is the art of systematically exploring and interpreting the external environment to better understand the nature of trends and deep drivers of change and their likely future impact on your organisation. It is the foundation for high quality strategic thinking that informs the development of futures ready strategy for an organisation.

Finding change that matters occurring in your external environment is what enables you to build an understanding of your organisation's change ecosystem, the external space in which it operates on a daily basis. As the first step in your strategy process, it gives you information about what change is relevant for your organisation both today and into the future. It also informs thinking about how to develop and implement possible responses to that change before it become a reality and your only option is to react.

Most organisations will be able to talk about their environmental scanning, although approaches vary between individuals and organisations. Even though it is a well-known activity, it is doubtful whether there is a common understanding of just what environmental scanning is. Many people think that reading the newspaper is scanning, while others think that networking with colleagues at a conference is sufficient to say they have done an environmental scan. Others think that scanning has a short term focus around what is happening today whereas my definition of scanning always starts with taking a long term perspective of change.

While short term approaches and sources gather information about the environmental external to the organisation, they yield very limited information which is not already in the mainstream, and its quality is limited to the quality and credibility of the source. Remember too that people doing the scanning need to be aware of the ways in which their own worldviews condition their scanning, and the risk of missing critical or otherwise useful pieces of information simply because their habitual ways of filtering information and cognitive biases do not allow them to 'see' that information.

During his time as a Strategic Foresight Analyst at Swinburne, Joseph Voros edited a number of scanning publications. The text below, reproduced with his permission, is extracted from an FAQ he prepared to explain the purposes of one particular publication, the Foresight Snippets, and explains the value of scanning in strategy development.

> *By definition, strategic scanning involves looking for what are known, in the foresight profession, as "weak signals." And because they are weak signals, they may seem to have little or no bearing on "here and now" and may therefore not seem useful (when seen from within the context of the hurly-burly of our day-to-day rush to do our daily work).*
>
> *The judgement of "usefulness" arises as a result of the (mostly unconscious) filtering of the world which we all undertake most of the time we are awake. This filtering process is certainly very important –it stops us from becoming overwhelmed by detail and data. But this filtering process also creates what are known as "blind spots" in our view of the world. We each have different filters operating and therefore we each have different blind spots. In an organisational setting this collection of blind spots can have disastrous implications for strategic thinking and strategy-making – just read some of the optimistic business plans for companies which were making slide rules in the late 1950s, for example!*
>
> *In essence, the job of strategic scanning is to interrupt our daily thinking, break us out of routine views of the world and how it may be changing, and, frankly, to smack up against some of the blind spots which we all possess.*

I do talk about the value of scanning whenever I have the chance. To use foresight effectively, the quality of your scanning must be high. There is in my view a 'garbage in, garbage out' effect with scanning. Depth in the practitioner is needed to produce depth and meaning in scanning output. Chapter 7 provides more detail about how to do scanning in practice and covers these topics in more detail.

Analytic Methods

Input methods generate a lot of information about change most often in the form of scanning hits or trends. Analytic methods are then used to make sense of that information for the organisation and its context. The question asked here is what seems to be happening. It is the stage where you look for patterns across disparate information sources and determine how to present them in ways that work for your organisation.

Figure 9 shows my interpretation of the life cycle of change (based on the work of Graham Molitor, Everett Rogers and Wendy Schultz). It shows that all change emerges at the periphery as an emerging issue before moving to the trend space and on to mainstream. The point here is that scanning needs to focus on all three areas – emerging issues, trends and mainstream to achieve a more comprehensive coverage of change shaping the organisation's future.

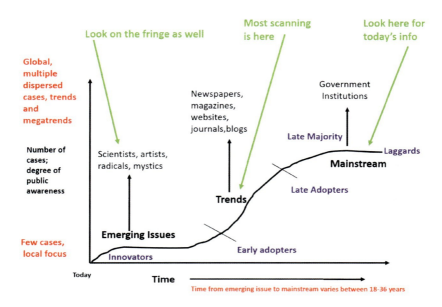

Figure 9: Life Cycle of Change

Mathews & Wacker (2003) extend this cycle to the downward curve beyond where trends are in the mainstream and have been socially accepted. They suggest a trend can move to cliché (generating amusement), icon (providing a model), archetype (regarded as a standard setter) and then oblivion, where the market for the trend returns to the few and the local. In a foresight sense, these latter stages are interesting because while impact is waning, there may still be short term strategic opportunities in these spaces. I also have a sense that extending the change cycle in this way suggests that the cycle is universal and that all change follows this pathway, but that's not the case. Trends have no fixed pathway into the future so view the lifecycle as a useful tool to help you understand where to scan to get most value for your organisation.

I use the term 'fringe' in Figure 9 but Hagel, Seely Brown and Davison (2010) pointed out the difference between 'fringe' and 'edge' which I now accept is an important distinction. They see fringes as marginal and of little value, they don't scale and impact on the mainstream is low or non-existent. Edges are the place where "unmet needs intersect with unexploited capabilities." They suggest that "edges that are destined to transform the core … often consist of a cadre of people with an intense aspiration to scale their innovations in order to make a difference in the world". The edge then is where the seeds of the future in the present can be found. I think that scanning the fringe might still be useful to explore what's happening but change here is unlikely to build over time and is largely invisible to mainstream society. Change that does strengthen becomes visible at the edge and can then be tracked.

I make the point elsewhere in the book that language is important so I'm heeding my own lesson here. Fringe is the wrong word. Emerging issues and change appear at the periphery, at the edge.

Trend Analysis

Trend analysis is a well-known analytical tool and can be quantitative and/or qualitative. It should be contextualised in the environment that has produced the trend. In foresight work, trends are not the end game, but one input into deepening our understanding of the change ecosystem that includes changes at a number of levels – personal, local, national and global. Trend analysis is about mapping the change ecosystem.

Using hindsight and foresight is useful when you are doing trend analysis. Analyse the connections and trajectory of the trends you are exploring in the past for as long as you want to explore how they might play out into the future. If your future time horizon is 20 years, then explore the trends and predecessors for 20 years into the past to see how they have developed over time. This will generally avoid the tendency to anchor your thinking about the future on your experience of the present.

Remember too that trends do not exist in isolation. They exist in your organisation's change ecosystem with connections and influencers and disruptors. Many trends might share a similar context and you will miss this if you analyse them separately. What is useful in your analysis is looking for the new and unexpected in that ecosystem and whether you would need any particular circumstances to exist for the trend(s) to develop further or decline in strength. Of course, you should also be looking for trends that challenge your current strategy.

Trend watching and analysis is big business. There are many people and organisations that will sell you trend reports for a lot of money with the analysis already done for you. These can be useful as a starting point but there are negatives. They have generic content about change in particular areas, have not been customised for your organisation's context and you need to trust the people or organisation doing the scanning. Ultimately you will need to assess relevance of the content for you organisation as part of your analysis.

Emerging Issues Analysis

While trend analysis is looking for issues that are gaining or declining in strength, emerging issues analysis seeks to identify change at the periphery that has not yet emerged fully - and that you believe will develop into an issue likely to affect your organisation in the future. This is where you will delve into the fringe where what you are finding seems a bit weird or ridiculous. Equally, issues that are disturbing or provocative should not be dismissed because they do not 'fit' with current management wisdom and worldviews.

Molitor (2003) identifies three stages of development for emerging issues:

- the emergence of the issue as an insight or idea on the edge that leads to some form of innovation – at this stage, these ideas can be ridiculed because they are so different to the mainstream,
- the issue is recognised by change agents such as social activists, think tanks, academics and further developed, moving it along the lifecycle towards the trend space – at this stage the issue is beginning to challenge status quo thinking, and
- over time, the issue becomes a mainstream concern and is resolved in some way; at this stage public interest wanes.

Assessing whether emerging issues are valuable in your analysis will more often than not cause you to hit an assumption wall. It's easy to dismiss an issue at the edge because it's not fully formed and its relevance is not yet fully apparent. A few questions to consider if do hit the wall: Does the issue change status quo thinking? If this issue continued to emerge, would you have to respond to it? What might be the best time to introduce this issue into the organisation? How can you write about the issue so that people accept it is important to consider? The aim here is to make sure you don't omit something that if ignored at this stage, might make your current business model obsolete in the near future.

Forecasting

All analytic methods are to some degree forecasting methods and can be both quantitative and qualitative. A quantitative approach has little value beyond the short term future, particularly if the outputs are framed as predictions. Framing those outputs as projections instead suggests something that is in the realm of probable futures, something that is likely to happen based on current knowledge. Demographic projections are an example of a forecast that seems to hold true over the long term – so far anyway.

Quantitative methods include extrapolation and econometric approaches, while megatrends are an example of qualitative forecasting. With any forecasting, there will always be blindspots involved, but to my mind the danger with quantitative methods is that they can be extrapolations of the past rather than explorations of the future. Qualitative approaches are perhaps better able to take account of blindspots in projections, particularly where entirely new paradigms emerge rapidly such as we are seeing in 2016 with the strengthening emergence of artificial intelligence. And remember that forecasting is not about predictions but rather about how connected trends might evolve.

Futures Wheels

This is a deceptively simple and powerful tool for exploring the implications of change having an impact on organisations. Developed by Jerome C Glenn in 1971 at Antioch Graduate School of Education, the tool explores the impact that flows from a trend (Figure 10). It projects possible cause and effect relationships between that trend and changes that are generated by it, as well as interrelationships across trends. Its use can synthesise thinking across a group and identify potentially unforeseen challenges and opportunities.

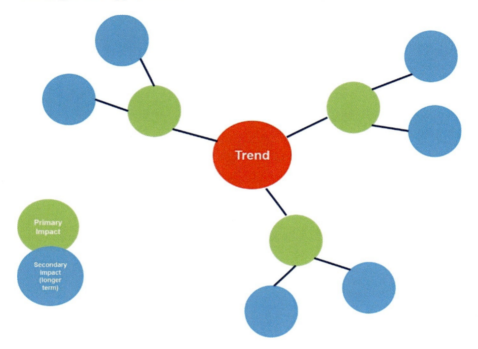

Figure 10: Futures Wheel

Futures Wheels can be developed over a number of impact levels. This is a quick overview of how to use them.

Step 1: write the name of a trend you want to explore in the middle circle. Describe it – for example, artificial intelligence becomes a reality across all work functions.

Step 2: brainstorm possible impacts of the trend across a range of domains – social, technology, economic, environmental, political, values. These are primary impacts. Put them in circles and connect them to the trend. *These are often impacts being felt today.*

Step 3: For each primary impact, brainstorm two or three secondary impacts. *These could be longer term impacts.* Put them in circles and connect them to the relevant primary impact.

Step 4: You can then work on each secondary impact in the same way to identify tertiary impacts.

Step 5: Look for connections between the impacts.

Step 6: Consider the implications of the map you have created – for policy, planning, opportunities, threats – how might you need to respond?

The Futures Wheel helps us move beyond linear, hierarchical thinking to see that change happens in a system, a network. It can provide a clear map of change shaping your organisation's future. Like all foresight tools, its use depends on the facilitator and the people in the room and the quality of thinking that emerges. And like all tools its use is designed to explore the possible rather than making predictions.

Three Horizons

Originally developed as the three horizons of business growth, the Three Horizons (Figure 11) used in a foresight context allow us to explore the shift from today's ways of doing things (Horizon 1) to consider emerging futures (Horizon 3) via transitional activity such as innovation (Horizon 2).

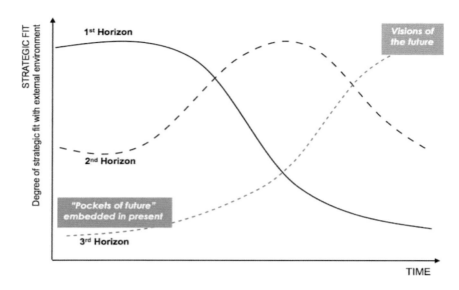

Figure 11: The Three Horizons (from Curry and Hodgson, 2008)

Horizon 1 is our way of operating day, the dominant system that becomes no longer fit for purpose as the world changes. **Horizon 3** is home to the 'seeds of the future in the present', the signals of change still on the periphery, that introduce new ways of working that could eventually replace those in Horizon 1. This space is comparable to where emerging issues have their origin.

Horizon 2 is the innovation/transition space, connecting Horizons 1 and 3 and exploring responses to change. Some innovations find homes in Horizon 1 while some are precursors to new ways of doing things that are emerging in Horizon 3. The three horizons are always present today.

As an analytical tool, the Three Horizons can be used to map out the state of each horizon today and the interrelationships between each – Horizon 1 as the current system, Horizon 3 as the desirable future state and Horizon 2 as the transition space, the disruption space. It can help us see beyond our linear view of the future, beyond the idea that time is one dimensional to a three-dimensional view where each of the three horizons has its own relationship with the future. This increases our ability to face to the future, to recognise that there is future potential in the present and to allow us to surface and explore the tensions between Horizons 1 and 3.

We need both these horizons for strategy development – organisations have to survive today as well as ensure a sustainable future. Sharpe (2013) points that out:

> ...we act with future intent all the time, linking what we are doing now to future outcomes. The central idea of the Three Horizons, and what makes it so useful, is that it draws attention to the three horizons as existing always in the present moment, and that we have evidence about the future in how people ... are behaving now.

Bill Sharpe's book *Three Horizons: the patterning of hope* (2013) is my bible for understanding the Three Horizons, along with a paper by Andrew Curry and Anthony Hodgson called *Seeing in Multiple Horizons: Connecting Futures to Strategy* (2008).

Interpretive Methods

At this stage, the focus is on interpretation of meaning for your organisation's context. What is important is again to not dismiss information without careful exploration – what seems unimportant today may be very important in the future. At this stage, you may also choose to involve people from outside your organisation who are sceptics and who can help surface the 'undiscussable' assumptions that underpin organisational decisions and action. The question asked here is: what's really happening? and the focus is what's happening beneath the immediately apparent. The aim is to challenge the categories of analysis, to question and test the meaning of the information that has been analysed, to dig below the surface to begin to understand what deeper drivers of change and how your organisation might respond.

Depth and Layers

A key concept at this stage is that of depth and layers. For example, Richard Slaughter (2004) writes of four layers of futures work:

- pop,
- problem-oriented,
- critical, and
- epistemological.

Pop futures work is superficial and media friendly and as Slaughter describes it: "eminently marketable, but largely bereft of theory or insight". This is the realm of the 'techno-wow' we see in Sunday newspaper magazines. Problem-oriented futures work has a practical focus, addressing issues of immediate concern. Most strategic foresight work occurs here. Critical and epistemological futures work look at the deep assumptions underpinning action, moving beyond the obvious and superficial to look at the very foundations of social life.

Depth in the practitioner is also a factor in the quality of interpretation. This includes understanding your own worldviews and your ability to accept opposing perspectives about a topic as valid until proven otherwise. The ability to move between levels of depth in your work, such as moving between pragmatic and progressive foresight domains is also important in matching the method to the context in which you are working.

Causal Layered Analysis

Causal Layered Analysis (CLA) was developed by Sohail Inayatullah (2004). He writes that CLA draws from poststructuralism, macro history and postcolonial multicultural theory. It is a method that aims to create spaces in which alternative futures can be explored by exploring the meanings we give to data and information, and its cultural 'boundedness'. There are four CLA levels:

- litany,
- social causes,
- discourse/worldview, and
- metaphor or myth.

CLA starts with the most visible and obvious beliefs and assumptions about a problem or issue, and then probes beneath the surface to explore underlying causes, worldviews and myths. This allows alternative solutions to be identified in ways that might not have been possible if the litany had been the only level of analysis. Figure 12 shows these four levels of CLA, and the move from short-term and visible factors to long-term and hidden foundations of our thinking. The litany is the most visible – the tip of the iceberg. It is where most conventional management approaches 'live', and is the home of newspaper headlines and media reporting. Phenomena at this level require little analysis to understand and are often accepted without question.

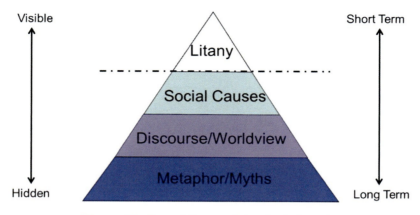

Figure 12: Causal Layered Analysis Levels

Beneath the **litany** are the social causes of the problem being explored, and may be documented through statistics, or quantitative analysis. **Causes** can be attributed to social, technological, economic, environmental or political factors. At this level, assumptions underpinning the analysis of the problem are questioned.

This questioning takes place at the **discourse/worldview** level, where individuals' often contested belief systems and mental models underpinning meaning are surfaced. This is where multiple perspectives and potential multiple alternative solutions emerge.

Metaphor/myth is the deepest level where work focuses on images and stories and taps into myths that enable and constrain the future being discussed. The final stage is to work backwards from the Metaphor/Myth level to reconstruct the issue and develop a new and shared perspective and how to address it effectively.

The value of CLA is that it takes us deeper into the assumptions and worldviews underpinning thinking and action than most empirical work. It challenges us to consider alternative perspectives and to explore how we might re-conceive an issue in ways that we had not considered previously and to identify potential solutions.

Prospective Methods

Prospective methods are both a critical step in strategy development and the most creative. Because we are exploring the future we are less constrained in our thinking, and we are able to create images of potential futures in which we can test our strategy, ask 'what if' questions, and take risks without having to live with the consequences. While it is creative and fun to play around in the future though, the most important part of using prospective methods is to use the output to strengthen our decision making today. Any prospective method that does not include a step that doesn't connect the future with the present should be treated with caution.

Visioning

Visioning is a well-known prospective technique, often used in community-based futures work because it is a highly participatory approach. See, for example, work done by the MAPP – Mobilizing for Action through Planning and Partnerships – a community-wide strategic planning tool for improving community health. But, as Wendy Schultz (1996) writes:

Currently the term is in danger of becoming clichéd, hackneyed, and over-used to meaninglessness: in an age of transition, vision is desperately sought but seems so elusive that the seeking itself is often ridiculed.

Visioning can surface the hopes, fears and beliefs of individuals about the future. The process seeks to answer questions such as 'what sort of future do we want', whereas scenario thinking explores questions such as 'what might happen in the future?' Visions can be very personal and underpin preferable futures – this is the future I want to happen – whereas scenarios deal with probable and plausible futures. With both methods, linking the vision of the future to action today is a critical step.

In conventional planning terms, people often get vision and mission confused. A vision is where an organisation sees itself in the future. It is aspirational and may never be achieved fully in the present. It continues to provide a future point of reference that can be used to inform decisions about the mission, which is primarily about what an organisation does in the present or short term future. In planning exercises, people often sit around and brainstorm questions like 'what is our vision?' While this might come up with useful outcomes, like any exercise it will probably come up with better outcomes if a structured approach is used.

Experiencing the Future

Exploring future possibilities using games, artifacts and immerse experiences is becoming a popular way of helping people think beyond today. There on online games usually run by foresight organisations around a particular issue. These can open to anyone anywhere in the world who wants to participate or closed, run for a particular organisation. The Institute for the Future is a good example of a foresight group who have this approach in their toolbox.

Experiential futures is another development at the intersection of foresight and design, one that focused on developing experiences for people to imagine possible futures, moving from the rational to the emotional and felt experience of what the future might be like. Raford (2012) describes this approach:

> *Highly visual, often emotional, and ethnographically infused, their approach brings the future alive through videos, objects,*

and print media. The result, they argue, is a profoundly engaging experience that goes beyond technical reports and PowerPoint presentations towards a new level of engagement.

Stuart Candy remarks that our imaginations are not temporal, they are not bounded by time and also points out that we lack strong public imagination about the future. The same could be said of organisations. Using our imaginations to explore possible futures is something we can all do, as long as we accept that the 'unimaginable' is a construct of our times. Stuart has recently co-developed the Thing from the Future, a card game that "scaffolds imagination, strategic conversation and storytelling about possible futures", allowing players to imagine a future world and design a thing that serves a purpose in that world – in essence, "reverse archeology" (Candy 2015).

Using experiential futures approaches allows thinking about possible, plausible and probable futures to move from our heads and from paper into artifacts that we create and make 'real' today. Serious Play by Lego is another example – while it's described as a tool to enhance business performance and innovation, it can and is used to create future scenario worlds.

Scenario Thinking

Scenario thinking has a number of well-defined processes for creating alternative futures that have been described and developed by many academics and practitioners since the 1960s. There are a range of approaches but at its core is the generation of a range of alternative future scenarios for an organisation, usually focused around particular strategic issues.

My first piece of advice here is to please don't just read a book and then run a scenario thinking exercise – it will be fun, but it will be ad hoc and superficial unless you are a very experienced facilitator. It would be better to get some formal training in the method or employ a good practitioner, or both. It looks deceptively simple to do, but the potential enhancement of thinking that can emerge from scenario thinking is often impossible to achieve by inexperienced practitioners. You need to take care selecting a scenario thinking consultant or firm. You need someone who is committed to the method, rather than using it as a commercial tool.

Richard Slaughter (2004) has critiqued scenario *planning* using an integral frame by pointing out that it focuses too much on 'out there' – the right-hand quadrant tangible and empirical world - at the expense of 'in here' - the left hand intangible and unobservable space. This results in a focus on empirical elements at the expense of non-empirical factors, and the lack of a structured approach to challenge assumptions about current social reality.

Perhaps the most important thing to remember about scenario work is that the scenarios created are a tool not the purpose, a way to trigged new thinking. The scenarios described will never come true in the form that you create them but thinking about the implications of those sorts of possible futures will both expand your perception of possible strategic options.

It is the combination of process and the opportunity for people to reflect on their own worldview as they apply it to the scenario worlds being created that is the power of good scenario work. If the process dominates at the expense of changing how people think and challenging their assumptions, the result will hold little real value for strategy purposes. We also risk responses like 'well, we've tried scenarios once, and they don't work' – which is what one deputy vice-chancellor said to me when I indicated we were thinking about using scenario thinking. Scenarios that reinforce the status quo and don't allow people to move into new thinking spaces are recipes for failure.

Notwithstanding these warnings, scenario work done well is challenging and creative, it can expose participants to novel information and new ways of thinking about issues, identifying blindspots and shifting thinking beyond the conventional. Remember the bottom line is they are a tool, not an outcome.

Figure 13 shows the different types of scenarios that can be developed. This classification is adapted from the work of Ged Davis (2002), then at the Shell Corporation.

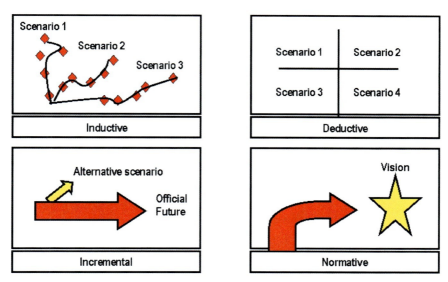

Figure 13: Types of Scenarios

Inductive scenarios emerge organically from discussion and exploration of drivers and trends, while deductive scenarios choose two or more of those drivers to define parameters for scenario worlds. Incremental scenarios are similar to the official future – the one written in our strategic plans – but different enough to move the organisation in a different direction, while normative scenarios are the realm of visioning and values – these are the futures that we believe **should** happen and the ones we work to make happen. All are valid depending on the context and outcomes that are needed.

Figure 14 shows the five basic steps involved in deductive scenario thinking. This is only one way to develop scenarios and I use it mainly because the process is usually quickly understood by participants in workshop situations and allows them to move to new thinking spaces quite readily.

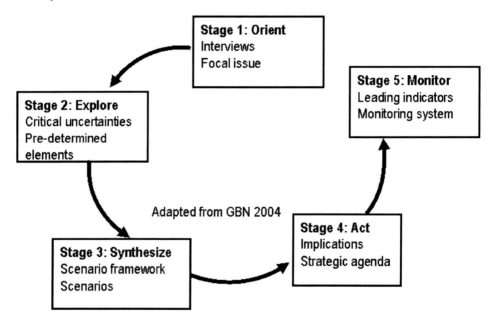

Figure 14: Basic Scenario Thinking Process
Adapted from Scearce and Fulton, Global Business Network, (2004)

While the exact detail will probably vary from practitioner to practitioner, these are the basic steps in a scenario thinking exercise.

Stage 1: determine a focal issue or critical decision to 'anchor' the process as well as the organisational assumptions that will aid or constrain your understanding of your focal issue.

Stage 2: identify and analyse internal and external driving forces affecting the decision (these drivers are usually categorised into 'predetermined elements', those which we have a good idea about how they will play out over time such as demographics and 'critical uncertainties', those which we have no real understanding about how they will develop into the future). This is the opportunity to challenge conventional wisdom in the organisation and explore what you don't know you don't know.

Stage 3: build scenario worlds (using inductive or deductive approaches) – this involves thinking about how the future might evolve for your organisation, industry and world. It includes creating scenario narratives that describe what it's like to live and work in these futures and how your organisation would be successful in each space.

Stage 4: identify robust potential strategic options and implications, and determine strategic options. This is done by putting yourself in the scenario and thinking about what it would be like to work in this environment – what would your options be? How would you be responding to your focal issue/decision? What new capabilities have emerged in these worlds? Where are the gaps today?

Stage 5: identify drivers and other issues that need to be monitored over time. These are often called 'early warning signals' that will allow you to see whether something identified in a scenario is 'coming true' or is less likely to happen. This last step is often neglected but helps to operationalise your scenario outcomes in the present.

More recent ways to develop scenarios that give you a head start in terms of identifying change within possible contexts include the Mobility VIP Cards, developed by the Art Centre College of Design in the USA. These cards give you one set that describes your future context and another set that describe the design context (customer, products, solutions). The aim is to create future scenarios rapidly and while originally developed for design thinking, they have great value for thinking about the future in new ways and focusing your attention on what will work for your organisation in that future.

Backcasting

As already mentioned, one of the dangers of scenario work is that the scenarios themselves will be treated as the end product when they are just the beginning of the real work of strategy development. We risk ad hoc, second rate outcomes that cannot be used by an organisation if the process does not include a backcasting stage that overtly links your identified future strategic options with today's strategic decision-making.

Backcasting is a way to link the future to the present to operationalise your scenario outcomes. It is done after you have identified potential strategic options as part of Stage 4 of scenario development. Starting in your preferred future, you work backwards to the present to understand events and decision points that might have occurred to create that future. You ask questions around what is happening, what caused the world to arrive at this point, what's not happening that is the previous stage, and how are you responding. In contrast, forecasting projects and roadmaps tend to project out from today into the future and risk taking the status quo into the future. Backcasting ensures that strategic decision making and the pathway to your strategic destination that is informed by the future.

Marcus Barber (Looking Up, Feeling Good) has developed a backcasting process that he describes as 'linking a vision to the future, to current operational choices using incremental time stages' and suggests it is often the missing link in scenario work. He's right. His process allows you to identify events/developments that could be critical decision points and lets you decide what to act on now and what you can wait to see how the event/development emerges.

Finally

No one method is enough in foresight work. Each level of the Generic Foresight Process Framework will need its own method(s) because the mode of activity is different at each level and no single method addresses each of those activities. The methods outlined in this chapter give you a starting point, remembering there are many more to choose from to ensure you get what works for your organisation. Try to avoid staying wedded to one or two methods as well, since new methods and new combinations of methods continue to emerge. The next two chapters provide information on how to do scanning and strategic thinking. The degree of futures readiness of your strategy is dependent upon the quality of these two activities.

7 Using Foresight: Environmental Scanning

Defining Environmental Scanning

Environmental scanning is used to enhance the depth and breadth of information about change that matters to your organisation and to identify early warning signals of issues that may need to be monitored over time. My definition of scanning is:

> *Environmental scanning is the art of systematically exploring the external environment for potential opportunities, challenges and drivers of change likely to have an impact of your organisation's future. Environmental scanning explores both mainstream challenges and wicked problems It identifies the new and emerging, as well as the known trends that are likely to affect an organisation's development in both the short and long term.*

Choo (1999) defines scanning as: 'The acquisition and use of information …about an organisation's external environment, the knowledge of which would assist … in planning the organisation's future course of action.' And Joseph Voros (2003) defines it:

> *By definition strategic scanning involves looking for what are known, in the foresight world, as "weak signals." And because they are weak signals, they may seem to have little or no bearing on "here and now" and may therefore not seem useful (when seen*

from within the context of the hurly-burly of our day-to-day rush to do our daily work).

All three definitions highlight the need to be searching the environment for indicators about change. The aim is to be ahead of that change with enough time to respond rather than following it and being surprised.

Different Scanning Modes

Most organisations have some form of environmental scanning in place and nearly all of us do some form of scanning on a day-to-day basis, particularly around our professional work. For strategy purposes however, environmental scanning needs to be formal and systemic and focused around particular problems, challenges or critical decisions being faced by the organisation.

There are many places to look for information about change: the knowledge held by staff, the organisation's competitive environment or market, the industry environment, and the broader social or macro environment. There are also different modes of scanning that vary in their usefulness for strategy development (Choo, 1999) as shown in Figure 15.

In undirected scanning you are reading a variety of publications/resources for no specific purpose other than to be informed. In conditioned scanning you are responding to information in terms of assessing its relevance to the organisation, looking for information about particular trends that you have identified as important for example. Informal scanning is an active information search about a topic but you are doing it a relatively unstructured way, while formal scanning uses formal approaches to obtain information for a specific purpose and to inform decision making.

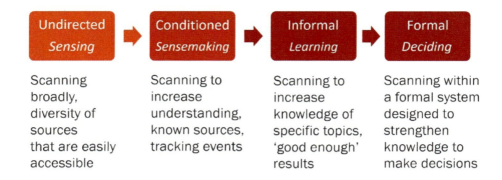

Figure 15: Scanning Modes

Scanning in a strategy context is **formal**, putting some structure into the process of obtaining information to prompt strategic thinking. It is much more than reading newspapers or industry journals, or checking the latest statistics about your market. It is about exploring both present certainty and future uncertainty and moving beyond what we accept as valid today. Without a structured approach to scanning, you will just be aimlessly scanning the web, and luck will be the only determinant of whether or not you find something useful.

A focus on formal scanning doesn't mean the other three forms of scanning are not useful. When you begin scanning, you will probably be in the undirected mode, getting used to what scanning is all about, and you may need to return there from time to time. As your skill increases, you will be using the other two approaches – conditioned to make sense of what you are finding, and informal to learn a bit more about specific topics. When you are scanning to inform a strategy process, you will have a focus and be scanning around that.

Getting Started

Setting up an environmental scanning system is like any project – it requires some planning before you 'go live' to ensure that the process is accepted internally and that you get the outcomes you need. Consider the following points as you set up your environmental scanning system.

Like everything to do with using foresight, organisational commitment is important. Do you have the support of your target audience and/or your manager to undertake the scanning? If not, is this important? If it is, you need to seek this support – at least in principle – before you begin. As with foresight in general, be clear about where scanning 'fits' into your existing strategy processes.

Understand for whom you are scanning. This is important so that your reporting meets their needs. What sorts of reports do they 'like' – in-depth, bullet points, two-page maximum, videos, graphics? What would a successful report look like (content, format, length)? Some suggestions for focus and format are made in the Reporting section later in this chapter. Consider this **before** you start scanning.

Identify the time frame for your scanning. To be successful, environmental scanning must scan well beyond today. Aim at least 10 years out, and don't be afraid to go out further. You are providing a long term context for your continuing strategy development so that you don't have to 'reinvent the wheel' every time you update your plan.

Establish a diverse scanning team. The exact number will depend on your needs and the size of your organisation. Be representative as far as necessary, and aim to include people who can think outside the box, who can lift their sights above day-to-day work and issues.

Remember to get a spread of desired personal characteristics for doing foresight (Chapter 1). Including 'outliers' and critics can be useful since they usually have a different and sometimes esoteric or extreme view on issues that could result in different interpretations, beyond the norm. You need this if you are to be able to challenge assumptions about why the way your organisation operates today may not be relevant and useful for much longer. The key criterion for selecting your scanning team is diversity across roles and perspectives.

Hold a briefing meeting for your scanning team to clarify the scanning process, get their views about topics to scan around, establish ground rules and expectations including how scanning 'hits' will be recorded and reported.

A Scanning Framework: Focusing Your Scan

Strategic scanning is of most value when it is focused or anchored around issues of current concern to your organisation. Alternatively, there may be a fork-in-the-road decision that needs to be made in the near future, and you need to get more information about potential implications of your options before you make a decision. An environmental scanning framework provides this focus to allow you to make the best use of your time and resources. Creating a framework clarifies what you are going to scan for and what is outside your parameters and why.

Take care here and make sure you are very clear about why you are choosing not to scan around particular issues, industries and geographies. Don't narrow your scope immediately so that you miss emerging issues. And remember that your worldview influences what you think is valuable scanning and what is not. Keep an open mind.

An **anchor** or framing question provides the focus you will need. Ask yourself what is changing and having an impact on the way you work. Why is this important? Current strategy will often provide a starting point since it will have identified a preferred future for your organisation – ask what is likely to influence how and when you might achieve that future? What do you need to know more about? What might disrupt that future? Spend some time thinking about this to identify what is really uncertain. Then, answer these questions:

- What is a key strategic issue you are facing now? Ensure this is strategic and long term, not operational and short term – put a future year into the question. This becomes the question you are trying to answer with your scanning.
- What do you need to know about (topics) the issue to be able to answer the question? This gives you a set of initial broad areas that you will be exploring in your scanning.
- How are these factors changing today and into the future? Your scanning will help you answer this question.

The questions should be uncomfortable for you because the answer should not be immediately clear. If you know the answer to the question, it's not the right focus for scanning.

Example Questions and Destination Year

These questions are adapted from client projects and provide some examples of the level of the anchor question you are trying to develop:

- How do we prepare for change (known and unknown) associated with ensuring a sustainable water future? (2025)
- What will our training services need to be to attract learners in 2020?

- What would enable Australia to successfully manage animal health in 2030?
- What do we have to do to achieve the best possible musculoskeletal health and wellbeing outcomes for our clients? (2025)

A Basic Scanning Framework

Table 6 provides some broad topic areas to explore using the STEEP framework (Social, Technological, Economic, Environmental, Political) as well as some generic areas that are focused on organisational operations. The table is generic enough to get you started but is not exhaustive and needs to be adapted by each organisation.

Table 6: Broad Topic Areas - adapted from: Global Business Network, Zpunkt Trenddatabase, www.z-punkt.de, Pitney Bowes Scanning Eyechart

STEEP Factor	Example Scanning Areas
Generic	Your industry and its operating environment Your services, and how they might evolve Your clients, and how their expectations might change Issues that are likely to affect your workforce and your staff, Emerging and converging technologies Emerging shifts in what we think is 'business as usual
Social	Demographics, population shifts, migration, generations Standards of living Value systems Socio-economic conditions Education Ethic/religious factors Crime, safety and security Family Health Attitudes to work and employment Leisure and lifestyle changes Consumer attitudes and opinions Fads and Fashions

STEEP Factor	Example Scanning Areas
Technology	Technology for service delivery
	Technological developments generally, including emerging technologies
	Convergence, competition and dependencies
	Nanotechnology
	Information and communications
	Technology legislation
Economy	All aspects of economic activity, global, national or organisations.
	Work and employment, occupations
	Consumer behaviour
	Globalisation
Environment	All natural factors
	Physical and geographical conditions
	Ecosystems
	Resources
	Sustainability
Politics	Often includes legal issues
	Global connections
	National factors

What You Will Find

When you are scanning, you are looking for indicators of change. You will find a range of content that tells you what is changing around your topics and how it might evolve over time. Here are some terms to help you understand what you are finding.

Driver of change/change forces: a major shift moving trends in certain directions, broad in scope and long term in nature (for example, globalisation); drivers of change usually cause either direct or indirect change of some sort in the environment in which they are operating.

Emerging Issue: an issue which has been deemed to be of potential future important and that has evidence of value and credibility building over time.

Event/Scanning Hit: a change happening in the internal or external organisational environment which can be observed and tracked, usually documented in a **scanning 'hit'**. It can be expected or a surprise.

Trend: a grouping/cluster of similar or related events that tends to move in a given direction, increasing or decreasing in strength of frequency of observation; trends usually suggest a pattern of change in a particular area (for example, consumer behaviour, technology use).

Weak Signal: Fuzzy, imprecise early indicator of a potentially significant event/change for your organisations, little evidence but considered to be worth tracking to test relevance.

Wildcard: low probability, high impact event that has the potential to be transformative in a short period of time.

These definitions aren't mutually exclusive – a scanning hit can be a trend or a weak signal for example. They give you a language to use when you are scanning and if these terms don't work for you, change them so that they make sense for your organisation.

Where to Start Looking

Chapter 6 showed the lifecycle of change (Figure 9). For scanning, the lifecycle can help you choose where you start looking for information about change.

The sources people use when they first start scanning are usually industry based. These are reports, newsletters, policy documents; they have wide acceptance as valid and as required reading if you are to stay informed about your industry. These are **mainstream** sources and you find them in your daily work – you already know what they are. Once you are comfortable with the scanning process, you should start looking for this sort of information outside your industry to see if there are cross-industry patterns emerging. What can you learn from these other industries that might be useful?

Identifying **trends** is relatively simple, mainly because they are generally labelled as such and there is much information about them (think about technological and demographic trends, generational issues). Because it is probable that the impact of trends is already being felt in the present, scanning is about deepening your understanding about how that trend might evolve over time and assessing relevance for your organisation. Remember too that in this space information is known; everyone has access to the same information. There's very little that is new in this space.

Identifying an **emerging issue** is more difficult. Emerging issues start with a value shift, or a change in how an issue is viewed. It's the single ripple of change that many people miss. An opinion leader or champion inevitably emerges who begins to move the issue into the public view and the change moves into the trend space. You might be looking at experts who are opinion leaders, or you might be looking at more edge sources such as those found in youth culture and social movements. This is where you find change that is so new, it can still be influenced in terms of how it is understood by others. By the time a hit has reached the trend space, the possibilities for influencing its trajectory are limited.

Weak signals are rarely labelled as such. You will usually have to make that judgement when something you see attracts your interest – at Swinburne, we used to say if you see the same thing three times in a short space of time in your scanning, it's working tracking. What you are finding though is not certain, has no clear form and you don't know whether it will matter for your organisation – but something is telling you to keep an eye on this shift even though at first glance, it can seem just a little too weird. This is your intuition at work – don't ignore it just yet.

Sources

Know that it is okay and necessary to look outside the box, beyond the mainstream, at the weird and the whacky, at what is emerging at the edge when you are scanning. This means that as well as identifying issues that are known, topical and relevant today you should also be looking far and wide for signals about how those issues might play out into the future and for signals of the new that is emerging, what isn't in your organisational worldview yet. You need to be curious. You need to be looking at industry and global levels.

For example, the future of work is topical right now and it covers a wide range of trends. Take one step back and look for connectors across those trends. What are the change forces that are shaping the future of work as a whole and across industries? In 2016, the digital imperative is an obvious one, along with artificial intelligence and the robots that are coming to the workplace. They are part of the story. What else is in the picture? What is familiar and what are you seeing for the first time? How are people reacting to the changes? What do organisations need to do to adapt to new ways of working? Think about what challenges and opportunities might emerge, and what decisions your organisation might have to make and when they need to make them.

Aim to scan across a wide range of sources. Here's some indicative sources (adapted from Shaping Tomorrow):

Newspapers, twitter, websites, blogs, wikis, podcasts, videos, news sites, newsletter, magazines, books, book reviews, presentations, reports, surveys, interviews, seminars, chat rooms, trend observers, advertisers, philosophers, sociologists, management gurus, consultants, researchers, experts, universities, journals.

There are also online tools you can use to identify useful content. These are all open and free resources and generally aggregate content for you around topics and sources that you choose:

- Flipboard
- Paper.li
- Pearltrees
- Pocket
- Scoop.it
- RSS Feed Readers: Feedly, Google Alerts, Mention, Warble Alerts

Use these tools to help you save time. These tools are developing all the time with new ones being developed quickly as technology continues to help us use information in new ways. Pick the ones that work for you – I use Flipboard and Feedly at the moment but a useful site is Shaping Tomorrow – their bot now automates the process to the stage where I am comfortable consolidating my sources there and letting it identify hits for me.

Starting to Scan

How do you decide where to start? You can simply do a keyword search around your topics and identify sources that look interesting. When you are doing this, look for these sorts of words used by Shaping Tomorrow that will help you identify what might be valuable.

New: novel, advance, innovation, renovation, fashion, latest, renew, innovate, newness, fresh.
First: inception, conception, initiative, beginning, debut, onset, birth, infancy, start, dawn, commencement.

Idea: notion, belief, apprehension, thought, impression, ideation, point of view, standpoint, theory, prediction.

Change: alteration, mutation, permutation, variation, modification, inflexion, mood, deviation, turn, inversion, subversion, forecast.

Surprise: marvel, astonish, amaze, wonder, stupefy, fascinate, dazzle, startle, take-aback, electrify, stun, bewilder, boggle, wildcard.

Opportunity: chance, opening, crisis, juncture, conjuncture, favorable, high time.

Threat: future, prospect, anticipation, perspective, expectation, horizon, outlook, look-out, coming, forthcoming, imminent, approaching, fear, uncertainty.

Unprecedented: no precedent, unparalleled.

When you find an indicator of change (trend/emerging issue), you can then:

- explore what the trend/emerging issue is doing today,
- explore what people are saying the trend/emerging issue will do over time,
- explore for ideas about the potential impact of the trend/emerging issue in your industry today and in the future, and/or
- place the trend in a global context and look for indicators of what is shaping it, what is pushing it to grow and what might be undermining it.

Richard Slaughter takes this set of questions to help you guide your scanning:

- What are the major driving forces?
- What big surprises are on the horizon?
- What are possible discontinuities (wildcards)?
- What are the sources of inspiration and hope?

Being able to scan well is a skill that builds over time. When you start, you are in what I call the **muddled** phase where you find a lot of things that look interesting, but you are unsure about how to judge their usefulness. You feel overwhelmed and it can all seem too hard. As your comfort level and skill increases, it is easier to determine what is useful and what isn't, and you start to see patterns across your scanning. This is the **building** stage. As a critical mass of people with scanning expertise increases you can move into the **analysis** stage where collaboratively you can work out what matters for your organisation, what to watch and what to act on.

Knowing When a Scanning Hit is Useful

Judging a hit as useful really depends on the filters you are applying to the assessment of the hit's value. While filters are important in scanning to stop suffering from information overload, filters can also be blindspots and biases. For organisations these blindspots and biases can have significant negative impact on strategic thinking and strategy development because the changes that could disrupt their industries and business plans will be missed or dismissed as irrelevant. As a general rule though, these questions (from Shaping Tomorrow) will help you decide whether a hit is useful or not.

- Does the hit help you to understand your issue better?
- Does it identify a new way of seeing the issue?
- Does it help you explore (rather than just accept) trends and their potential impacts?
- Does it identify and assess possible future threats and opportunities, including radical alternatives?
- Does it challenge existing assumptions underpinning current policies and practice?

Not all your sources have to be credible in the conventional sense. If what you are finding suggests that it may be relevant to your organisation then record it. That doesn't mean you have to report on it immediately – you can track it over time and report when you judge that people in your organisation won't reject the change as rubbish. Criteria for determining usefulness also varies depending on the scanning mode you are working in.

When you are scanning in Sensing mode you are exploring what's 'out there' and in this space, it's advisable to not use common measures of validity and credibility to assess the usefulness of your scanning hits, particularly when you are scanning at the edge. Schultz (2006) provides the following indicators of usefulness when you are scanning at the edge:

- **Credible**: little or no credibility (because it's unusual),
- **Documented**: little documentation (only one or two sources available),
- **Numerous**: statistically insignificant (there are few cases),
- **Accepted**: little or no consensus, refuted by conventional experts,
- **Theoretical**: defies existing theoretical base, and
- **Relevance**: scan broadly, outlier relevant, early signals.

In Deciding mode, where you are generating outputs to inform decision making, Schultz then indicates that you need different criteria:

- **Confirmation** – multiple citations across a range of sources emerging over time as more and more cases occur - validates existence of change and direction of trend,
- **Convergence** – emerging scientific consensus – new paradigms emerge, and
- **Parallax** – depth of field where views on emerging change gathered from many perspectives - ensures original perception of change is not an artefact of one culture or organisation.

I recommend you find this paper by Wendy Shultz – it will help you understand the differences between scanning and conventional research. The distinctions she makes are important as they will help you be more open in your response to scanning sources, and demonstrate that the scope of those sources and their value will vary at different times in the strategy development cycle. If you find something that might be useful you can:

- test it by searching for relevant keywords to see what sort of links appear; if you get a lot of hits and the quality of the hits seem high, it means the issue is being talked about by many people and it is something you should include as a scanning hit, or
- test it with your scanning team, or others in the organisation – does it seem important to them or should you track it for a bit longer? or
- if you think it's quite weird still, put the hit on a watch list, to see if it appears on your scanning radar again.

If you hit an assumption wall, remember to explore a bit further before dismissing what you have found as irrelevant. What else might happen that would make this emerging issue more likely? If nothing substantial comes from this further exploration, then this hit won't be something useful today but keep an eye on it. Something that seems irrelevant today could well become very relevant in five or 10 years.

Ultimately, your intuition will help you decide whether the hit matters. A strange thing to say perhaps but my definition of intuition is expertise + experience = intuition. It's informed judgement. You are scanning for the organisation and industry within which you work. You know its challenges and issues. You have particular skills and knowledge. You have a view about what works and what doesn't. You will have a perspective on what needs to change. If you are using foresight, you should have an open mind. As long as you take a big picture and long term view of changes you are finding and be alert to your worldview in assessing the value of scanning hits, then intuition is another way to you decide what is and is not useful.

Counter Trends and Wildcards

As well as looking for trends and emerging issues, you should also be alert for counter trends and wildcards. When you identify a trend, ask what the **counter trend**, the opposite trend might be. Do some scanning to see if such a counter trend is obvious – it might be but it might not be. If you find some evidence of a counter trend, record that and keep an eye on its development. Counter trends can derail a trend's future trajectory, and you need to be alert to potential alternative outcomes if the counter trend get stronger over time. **Wildcards** are those low probability, high impact events that have the potential to change the world overnight. They are often outrageous in the sense that they are more possible and probable than plausible for today's context. That's the point. Using wildcards in your strategic thinking requires an open mind. Here's an example from my practice.

> *I was working with a Board group for an educational institution in Australia, developing scenarios to help them explore their future. I walked around the room, asking someone at each table to pick a card from my pack of wildcard cards. I reached one table that had the Board Chair and some senior managers and asked them to pick a card. They picked the card that said: contact with extra-terrestrial life has been confirmed. The conversation then went something like this:*
>
> *"We don't want to do this."*
>
> *"Why?"*

"It's ridiculous. We should be focusing on what we can do not this sort of airy fairy stuff."

"Can you hang in there and do it anyway please?

"We don't want to do it."

"Please do it – it's part of the process and you'll see why when we've finished."

This group developed a marketing plan to attract aliens to their institution to study – this was a new student market for them, one that they had never considered before. Yet, they managed to produce quite a coherent marketing strategy. I was pleased.

When it came time to talk about strategic options, I looked eagerly to this table of people. They said they had nothing to add. I asked them about their marketing plan for aliens. They said it was rubbish, and they didn't want to use it. It wasn't rubbish, but nothing I said could convince them to think about how to apply their thinking to their situation today.

Wildcards by their very nature are improbable and even preposterous. Thinking about them takes you to places you wouldn't normally choose to explore, and you will need to resist the voice in your head that tells you that you that it will never have an impact on your work. Use the wildcard to explore questions like 'if this did happen, what opportunities or challenges would our organisation face?'

Recording your Scanning Hits

When you start to record your scanning hits, you are working at the **analysis** stage of the Generic Foresight Process (Figure 6). You are working out how to organise your scanning hits in ways that will make sense to your organisation. There are two main steps involved in this stage. First, you have to decide how you are going to store your scanning content and second, you need to know how you are going to categorise that content. No one wants to look down a long list of scanning hits in a report. Some form of categorisation and sorting will be needed.

Storing your Scanning Hits

You can record your hits manually if you are just starting out because you won't have many sources and few hits for a short time. If you are serious about scanning, you will need to find a way to store your content in the cloud, preferably with a platform that helps you make sense of what you are finding and allows you to share your scanning output. Sharing content across your organisation using an open platform opens up the possibility of everyone in the organisation being able to contribute to the scanning – after being appropriately trained/inducted/familiarised with how to scan and the parameters of the scanning task.

Evaluating a Scanning Platform

In this section, I provide some factors that you should take into account when you are deciding on a scanning platform for your organisation.

In terms of input, you need to be able to enter information as quickly as possible and the system needs to intuitive and easy to learn. With artificial intelligence emerging, it's not too much to expect that your platform will have automated this process for you to a significant degree. Ideally too, your platform will be an open and accessible system, to which many people are contributing, either from within your organisation or in a crowdsourced environment. While it's not essential your scanning platform should have some way of helping you analyse your content. At the basic level, the platform needs a good search function that lets you retrieve and report on your trends and issues when you need them in the format you need. Some platforms are specific purpose, allowing you to store your content while others will offer a range of analytical and reporting tools.

In terms of output, data visualisation is becoming mandatory, but reporting can also be written, video and other forms depending on the platform. Of course, cost will play a part. Most platforms will charge a fee while others will provide some functions for free. Finally, privacy of your data is a critical consideration – open platforms are useful for sharing and finding new content that you hadn't seen previously, but there will be circumstances when you want to keep your data private to your organisation.

What I Use

I have been using Shaping Tomorrow to store my scanning hits since around 2005. Before then I had explored a range of possible ways to store what I was finding but as the number of individual scanning hits increased, I realised an excel spreadsheet wasn't going to work anymore. I searched for online services and found Shaping Tomorrow. I now do work for them on occasion and pay for a basic private site because I believe their platform is one of the best in terms of being open, accessible and with a good range of tools for analysis and reporting.

The scanning process itself is now automated, so I put in my sources and Athena, their bot, finds me relevant scanning hits which I can edit, accept or reject. Instead of taking up to five minutes to enter a hit, I can do it now in 30 seconds and focus on analysis and interpretation. The people who run the site are very responsive and have spent a great deal of time incorporating the latest thinking about foresight into its design and functionality.

Of course, there are other ways to store scanning output and you need to decide what will work for your organisation.

Categorising your Hits

STEEP is a familiar way of categorisation your scanning hits – Social, Technological, Economic, Environmental and Political. There are many other systems that have been developed - PEST, PESTLE, STEP, STEEPLED - and all focus on the type of change you are finding. This is a well-used categorisation approach and can be introduced into your organisation very quickly – the terms are familiar and a lot of organisations use one of the variations.

VERGE (2004) was developed by Richard Lum and Michelle Bowman who were disenchanted with the STEEP approach. Their framework focuses on the point of impact across human systems rather than type of change and can be used to both identify where to scan and to categorise what you are finding. There are six categories in this system.

Define: The concepts, ideas, paradigms used to define ourselves and the world around us. Examples: worldview, philosophy, archetypes, religion, social values.

Relate: The social structures and relationships which define people and organisations. Examples: family and lifestyle groups, government, demographics, habitat and ecosystem, education.

Connect: The processes and technologies through which we create goods and services. Example: manufacturing, work force, biotechnology, wealth, engineering.

Create: The technologies that connect people, places, and things. Example: information technology, transportation, language, media, visual arts, space.

Consume: the way in which we acquire and use the goods and services we create. Examples: consumer preferences, modes of exchange, marketing, retail practices.

Destroy: the ways in which we destroy value why we do it. Examples: violence and killing, waste.

This is a useful way of looking at scanning because it forces you to move beyond the simplicity of STEEP. This is a somewhat more substantial scanning framework and you may find it useful in some situations and not in others. Your categorisation system needs to be one that you know will be understood quickly in your organisation and that will allow you to standardise the top level of your categorisation system to the degree that you need. Remember though, you are aiming to shake up thinking and that starts with your choice of categorisation system.

Recording your Hits

Recording a scanning hit provides you will the information you need to understand the change being described to a level where you don't necessarily have to go back to the original article. When you identify a hit that you want to record, capture the following:

- a title for the scanning hit,
- the source where you located the hit, and the date it was published,
- a brief summary of what it is all about,
- your view of the implications for your organisation, both positive and negative, and
- classification (STEEP, VERGE, keywords, or a classification system agreed within your organisation).

Figure 16 shows a sample of one of my scanning hits recorded on my Shaping Tomorrow scanning site. The title is linked to the original article, the major change that matters is summarised as well as your assessment of implications. The tools underneath the *Implications* section are designed to both categorise and analyse your hit.

WILDCARD: THE FALL OF UNIVERSITAS

Maree Conway ◎ 23 October 2015 ▶ Copenhagen Institute for Future Studies

What is changing?

As our notion of work continues to change, there is increased pressure put on education systems to boost their relevance. Generation of change. However, we are already beginning to witness the tides of change in an emerging class of young urban creatives - a slice of Generation Y - who are intent on being equally as successful as previous generations, only in their own way.

Implications

Increasingly, the industrialised education systems of the 20 th century are being criticized for producing a skills mismatch and failing to reflect the new and evolving requirements of the labour force in a 21 st century economy. The challenge for universities lies in adapting to the changing needs and expectations of a knowledge society powered by decentralised networks, hyper-individualisation and technological development.

Tags: Education, Knowledge, Learning, Unifutures

Figure 16: Example Recorded Scanning Hit

Over time, you will recognise common or similar patterns of change across your hits. At this stage you probably have a trend and you will be able to write a short summary statement about that trend so that people will understand its importance to your organisation. Questions about the trend's implications for your organisation will also probably start to emerge at this stage too – keep a note of these questions as they will be useful at the analysis and reporting stage. You may also start to see connections (both positive and negative) among trends and some platforms allow you to store these connections.

Analysing Your Scanning

You will now have a repository of trends that your scanning team think might be important to your organisation's future. The next stage in your scanning process is to analyse your trends and test their relevance for your organisation's future. You are looking for what you need to pay attention to now, what you need to watch in the medium term, and what you need to monitor over the long term.

The Change Ecosystem

The change ecosystem is the name I use to describe the space in the external environment where you will identify indicators of change that are predominantly in the form of trends. You will be or should be, identifying trends that can help people in your organisation understand the depth and breadth of change that is shaping its future. The critical element once you get to this stage is to understand that trends don't exist in isolation. You will have already started exploring how your selected trends might evolve over time when you scanned. Now you are also looking at a number of trends to see how they connect, collide and intersect with each other. There could be weak or strong connections between trends. Wildcards and other discontinuities might intervene and derail a trend trajectory completely. Systems thinking principles are useful here.

Trends aren't fixed. They may have some form of a lifecycle but that doesn't mean they have certain outcomes. Marcus Barber calls them 'tendencies' because change is tending to take a particular direction, but it may not always be so. Not all trends will go through a complete lifecycle. They can have a range of outcomes depending on how they intersect with each other. Trends that seem certain today may well be irrelevant in five years. No trend has a fixed trajectory into the future and the further into the future you look, the more potential pathways there are.

You need to explore those alternative pathways to see whether your view that this trend is important to your organisation will remain robust irrespective of how the trend evolves. Ask questions such as 'if this trend continues to develop in this way':

- might it cause a fundamental change to the way your organisation delivers its services?
- might it generate fundamental change in how your industry is organised?
- might it make our business model no longer sustainable?

The existence of multiple pathways for trends is why ad hoc or once off scanning is of little value. Trends identified in a single scan may wane in strength very quickly, so any decisions made about how to respond to the implications of that trend or trends in the short term could be flawed. Similarly, emerging issues that are ignored or discounted because there isn't enough information to validate them using conventional criteria can cause that surprise event no one saw coming.

Trends are not set in stone so don't reify them. Track them, assess them, judge them for relevance. Consider how they interact in the change ecosystem you are dealing with. And remember, there will always be another trend coming over the horizon that will matter to your organisation. Remember too that an over-dependence on trends could well trap you in the present since the change embodied in trends is with us today. You may well miss the complexity of the change ecosystem that is a mix of weak signals, trends and wildcards and constrain thinking about the future to trends rather than the full gamut of change.

You are still in scanning mode at the moment, rather than developing alternative futures or considering strategic options. What you are doing is looking for patterns across your scanning that indicate something could potentially disrupt how your organisation operates today or in the near future, trends that might be critical in terms of your organisation's sustainability. You are looking for possibilities, for questions, for challenges to the conventional.

What is Important Now and What Can Wait

Your scanning analysis will also need to make an assessment of the likely impact of your identified trends over your scanning period. When it seems right, I use a Trend Relevance Assessment guide that I've adapted from a system Shaping Tomorrow developed – it's one way of assessing relevance of your trends for your organisations. The assessment covers a number of categories:

- Timeframe: *when will a mainstream impact begin to appear?*
- Scope: *how widely will the trend be accepted/adopted?*
- Impact: *how strong will the impact of this trend be?*
- Likelihood: *how quickly might this trend have an impact on the organisation?*
- Urgency: *what is the required speed of response by the organisation to the trend?*

The first three relates to the trend itself, the last two relate to the impact of the trend on the organisation. Each category can be allocated a number between 1 and 5 that when combined across categories will give you an Importance Score. You will need to determine the cut-off point for each of the decision categories that suits your organisation, but as a guide:

- assessments between 20-25: **act now**
- assessments between 15-19: **manage**
- assessments 14 and under: **watch**

People who are familiar with risk assessment and management will recognise this structure. You could use this with a single trend if it is critical to your organisation or a group of trends. This sort of quantitative, scoring approach won't work in all situations so you will need to judge when to use it. You are aiming to explore implications of the trends you have identified to assess relevance for your strategy in the near (act), medium (manage) and long term (watch).

The process of analysing your scanning hits for relevance for your organisation is a pivotal step in environmental scanning. This is a step where you add your judgement and perspective to the mix, and where you add meaning in the context of your organisation's strategic focus and priorities.

Reporting

Reporting enables you to share your scanning analysis. The form of your output will depend on the timing of your strategy cycle and whether you are using reports for a specific purpose or as a way to raise awareness about foresight. Reports can be in the form of one page briefs, detailed reports or anywhere in between. You can produce workshop reports, videos and glossy publications. What is important is that people who did not do the scanning must be able to accept your content as credible and understand the nature of the analysis that has led to your findings. It's not just about the output, but also the analytic steps and thinking that occurred that needs to be reported.

In any report you produce make sure you include a statement that makes it very clear that the scanning hits and trends are not predictions. The analysis you are providing is an assessment of the importance of the changes being reported for your organisation's strategy. Your report must therefore be designed to inform thinking about how the organisation might need to respond to increasing complexity and uncertainty in its external environment. As well as demonstrating relevance to your organisation, your report also needs to disrupt conventional thinking – a simple way to do this is to add some provocative trigger questions to help people move to a different thinking space.

People will gravitate to the familiar in your report, to what supports their thinking. To balance this, include findings from all stages of the change lifecycle – emerging issues, weak signals, trends and mainstream developments, as well as cross-industry and global change both short and long term. While people may not immediately accept what is for them new and strange, not letting in new and uncomfortable information because it doesn't fit with existing culture and mindsets is a recipe for eventual failure. Continuing exposure to information about what's changing is an awareness raising activity that may help people recognise the need to adapt their thinking to be futures ready.

Types of Reports

There are different types of report you can produce. Here are some examples:

- a snapshot report of the external environment,
- a background paper for the strategic planning cycle,
- regular trend reports on selected trends,
- more detailed quarterly reports on implications of trends and drivers, and/or
- quick snippets about what you are finding (like the Swinburne Foresight Snippets).

When you are writing the report, consider these questions to help you organise your content:

- what impact might this change have on your organisation today and in the future?
- does the change help you understand what's influencing how you do what you do today?
- is the change potentially going to disrupt your operations in the future, but how is not clear?
- what might be the implications for your organisational strategy?
- what are you options for responding today?

The following section describes three types of report that can be produced to communicate the outcomes of your scanning process. These reports aim to keep your scanning visible in your organisation and to achieve this, you need to ensure relevance. The exception is the scanning hits report which really is designed to be an awareness raising report and highlight what is going on 'out there' in the external environment. These three forms are suggested as a starting point; you will need to design the specifics of your own reports to suit your organisation's culture. Remember too that you may need to produce several outputs to suit different audiences.

Scanning Hit Reports

This is a regular report on what you are finding – the Foresight Snippets (Chapter 2) we did at Swinburne is an example. It's a list of interesting/relevant things you have been finding in your scanning. There's usually little formal analysis.

Your report can be sent out via email (although this has the potential to annoy people whose inboxes are overflowing), or via a website that also allows staff to access them and even rank the hits on relevance/importance to your organisation's strategy. The latter will obviously cost money to develop, but it allows a degree of interaction not possible with the conventional email approach. One advantage with the website is that staff can check it when they have time, rather than having to keep track of emails. Where appropriate you could also use this site to create a first draft of your report by using staff ratings to identify issues to include.

Trend Reports

Once you have done some work on initial interpretation of your scanning hits, you can prepare a trend report that you might produce monthly, quarterly or as needed. This could be simply your trend summary, assessment and implications that can be framed as questions to promote thinking and discussion. This report is more focused than your scanning hits report, and has a higher credibility rating than individual scanning hits. There are many uses for such a report – for example, general interest, targeted discussion at meetings, planning workshops or forums to address specific change.

Strategy Reports

A third type of report can be linked directly to the strategic development cycle. It is best produced to be a resource to groups and organisational units to inform their thinking about what options they might pursue. This ensures that everyone in the organisation has the same information about the external environment and the change likely to affect the way they do business into the future. This type of report can also be used as an input into exercises like scenario thinking. It provides the starting point for explorations about what might happen and what is possible and plausible.

This report's content should include a summary of the implications of the changes you have identified earlier in your scanning process and focuses on the implications of that change for your organisation – what might it mean for strategy now and into the future? What needs to be acted on now, and what can be monitored over time? What must not be ignored?

The exact format of the report will depend on your organisational culture and ways of operating. At the very least, you need an executive summary that identifies very clearly the critical change your organisation needs to consider – busy people will expect this. In the early stages of developing this report, you might want to send the report to 'friendly' managers and seek their feedback. Amend your report as needed to provide additional information or clarification. You may be able to undertake a custom scan on a particular topic based on this feedback that can also demonstrate the value of scanning to particular people or groups.

One Organisational Scanning Process

Figure 17 shows one scanning structure established for a small non-profit organisation. A senior manager in this organisation had used environmental scanning previously and wanted to develop the capacity in her new organisation.

The critical factor that made this structure work was the people who were in the middle of it. They had open minds, they recognised the value of thinking about change shaping their organisation's future, they were curious, they wanted their organisation to survive and prosper in their field, they valued and respected everyone's opinion.

. This was a particular mixture of the intangible and the tangible that worked, producing engagement across the organisation. While the structure can be replicated, that particular mix of people and ways of thinking is much harder to copy and is the stronger success factor.

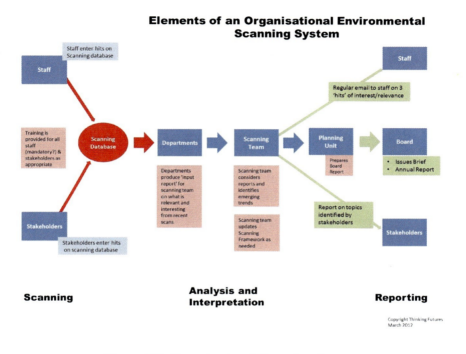

Figure 17: Organisational Scanning System

Finally

Scanning is about ensuring that there are no surprises in the future operating environment for your organisation – that is, avoiding organisational myopia. Scanning processes should always be designed to provide information to inform the development of flexible strategy that readies your organisation to respond quickly to the changing environment rather than react to it. In essence, the job of scanning is to interrupt our daily thinking, break us out of routine views of the world and how it may be changing and to remind us of some of the blind spots which we all have.

For scanning to be of any value in strategy development, it must be done on a continuing basis. It needs to be someone's job. You are aiming to build your understanding of the external environment in ways that are both broad in terms of sources and deep in terms of understanding of the issues found. You are looking for information to inform your organisation's strategy development processes that is useful, credible and challenging.

What you are trying to avoid is the 'head in the sand' syndrome where new information is locked out, where it's believed there is no value in exploring what might be coming over the horizon either because today is seen as more important or the prevailing culture is to think the future will be more of today. Or perhaps your organisation is trapped in data where predictions are the norm, or even worse where the future is left to one or two people to shape. Expect surprises with this way of thinking pervades your organisation and expect to stay reactive in your work.

You will find that your focus on what really matters sharpens over time. You will still be under the influence of the busyness syndrome on a daily basis but you will have clearer signposts about where to focus your scanning and how to use your output. Your biggest challenge is likely to be finding the time to scan and to think about what you are seeing – but you and your organisation must make the time if it wants to be proactive in responding to change. Your thinking will expand and you will be able to contribute to the development of a longer term view of your organisation's possible futures.

8 Using Foresight: Strategic Thinking

Defining Strategic Thinking

Strategic thinking is identifying, imagining and understanding possible and plausible alternative futures for your organisation, and using the knowledge gained to strengthen your thinking about your potential options to position your organisation effectively in the external environment in the future, in order to make better informed and more robust decisions about action to take today.

This is my definition and it is long. The length reflects the fact that strategic thinking is not a simple concept. It's the process of creating and exploring possible futures and using that knowledge in your organisational decision making. The key elements of the definition are the need to explore possible futures in your strategy process to identify potential opportunities and risks you want to avoid so that your strategy is robust and sustainable.

Other useful definitions are:

The way in which people in an organization think about, assess, view and create the future for themselves and their associates. It is more than responding to both day-to-day as well as long-term problems, opportunities and new realities; it is creating tomorrow. It is not reactive, but proactive... Strategic thinking

always involves change, and often, profound personal change
(Kaufman et al 2003:40).

A cognitive process ... that precedes strategic planning or action, whereby an individual contemplates the future development of the organisation whilst considering its attributes, its past and present and the external realities within which it operates (Tavakoli and Lawton 2005:6).

The last two definitions focus on one important thing: the individual thinking about the future. Strategic thinking is foresight in action; it happens within our minds. For our individual strategic thinking to be useful for strategy development, it needs to be surfaced and built as a collective capacity through the use of overt processes.

Two basic foresight principles are also highlighted in these definitions. One, thinking about the future does not discount the past and present, but it does require you to move beyond today's status quo. And two is the need to remember that the future is shaped by change, and understanding that change often requires us to challenge our worldviews, both as individuals and collectively. At its most basic, strategic thinking is putting your decisions today into their internal and external contexts over both the short and long term, before you decide on action to take.

Strategic Thinking in Organisations

Based on my work I see a range of ways in which organisations approach strategic thinking today. Many use **conventional** approaches to strategy that we have already covered in earlier chapters – scanning for change that is outsourced, a planning process that is largely formulaic, staff don't get consulted in meaningful ways and senior managers make all the decisions. Everyone else is expected to engage with the process without any say in final decisions. This approach is introspective, focusing on the organisation and its historic strengths and applying that to today's needs, and where one or two people think they know all the answers. They don't.

One point about this conventional space. Often people will say something like 'it's not my job to think about the future' or 'I'm not paid to be strategic' or 'I can't see how I would have permission to think strategically'. I understand these sentiments, and I know they are real, but see them as misguided. Foresight is first and foremost a state of mind. Everyone has a foresight capacity that can be surfaced and used in a conducive context, whether that is one you create, or one where you adapt existing processes. Logically, I know that ways to use foresight in individual workplaces are not always obvious, possible or easy to implement. I also know that resources and time to use foresight are often not available. Making statements like 'it's not my job to think about the future' however, risk you as an individual being trapped in the status quo.

The second type of organisational approach recognises that the world is changing rapidly and these organisations are **making an effort** to change how they develop strategy – they tend to make tweaks around the edges to existing processes, and nothing really changes. Conventional planning processes still dominate, although there is usually more staff involvement. These places are starting to look outwards but don't really know how to combine the external with the internal to integrate both into a more holistic and futures infused strategy development process.

Finally, some organisations understand the need for their strategy to be **futures ready** and start externally to understand in a very deep and considered way how the environment into which they need to 'fit' or position themselves is changing. They take their lead for strategy from the outside, and then work to adapt the internal parts of the organisation and its capabilities to be able to respond effectively to the shifting external environment. Staff are involved from the beginning, and strategy development is more fluid and flexible. There's not necessarily a fixed strategic plan but rather a continuing overview of the external environment and conversations that drive adjustment to strategy as needed.

Of course, the real situation is much more nuanced than this, but the point is clear. The difference among the three approaches is usually that futures facing organisations consider thinking about the future to be valuable and necessary work and make time and resources available to make sure that thinking happens.

Strategic Thinking and Conventional Business Thinking

Strategic thinking is essentially about changing the way we think about the future of our organisations. It is about moving beyond patterned responses and habitual thinking that no longer work well when uncertainty is dominant in our operating environments. It requires retraining our brains to see new things and to make new connections, to be creative by thinking beyond the status quo, imagining the possible rather than seeing only the tangible in front of us today. It is about moving our brains fromconventional business thinking to futures focused strategic thinking as described in Table 7.

Table 7: Characteristics: Conventional & Strategic Thinking Approaches

Conventional Business Thinking	Strategic Thinking
Immediate term	Depth of vision
Own business focus	Cross-disciplinary
Attention to detail	Broad vision
Techno-economic trends focus	Trends and emerging issues
Problem approach	Systems approach
Less attention to connections	Interactions and cross-impact
Continuity assumption	Wild cards and discontinuities
Bottom line focus	Strategic focus
Undiscussables are never spoken	Speak the unspeakable
Short term focus	Long term orientation

A single future	Alternative futures
Mainstream thinking	Mind changers
Past and present dominate decision making	Future dominates decision making

To make this shift, we need to understand the 'blinders' or cognitive biases that prevent us from seeing the signals of change in our environment (Day & Schoemaker 2005) which include:

- **mental filters** – our embedded and patterned responses to things we see in our worlds,
- **overconfidence** – we are far too certain about how the future will develop,
- **penchant for confirming** rather than disconfirming evidence – we do not look for ways to challenge what we believe to be true,
- **dislike for ambiguity** – we want certainty, and we certainly don't get paid for saying 'I don't know what to do', and
- **group think** – the Abilene effect, or members in a group 'going along' with a group decision, and not speaking up to challenge that decision, even though no one in the group agrees with the decision.

These are only some of the cognitive biases which affect our thinking, both as individuals and collectively when we come together in organisations. Reflect on which ones you have and which ones your organisations might display – and the implications of those biases for your strategy development.

If you are serious about building a long term context for your strategy by using strategic thinking more effectively, then you need to be aware of your cognitive biases so your thinking is not constrained to the degree that you miss something important. And, so that when you hit an assumption wall, you challenge your thinking automatically. Any processes you use must also identify ways to alert people to these biases – that is a non-negotiable design point. Asking simply 'why do you think that?' is often enough to start a reflection on the assumption at work in someone's brain.

As an aside, when someone hits one of their assumption walls and resists the need to challenge their thinking, consider that when they say 'I don't believe that' or 'that's rubbish' they really mean 'I have no proof that fits my worldview that enables me to accept this as true, nor am I inclined to look for a means to enable me to accept this'. Your job is to find a way that helps move them towards acceptance.

Taking Time to Think Strategically

Strategic thinking requires time to be set aside on a regular basis to think and talk collaboratively about change that is coming over the horizon, how it might affect your organisation, what your possible responses are and when you might need to take action. This stage is about identifying the widest range of possible and plausible strategic options rather than replicating today's strategic options so you need many perspectives. It's the divergent thinking stage of strategy development and is the time for strategic conversations.

It's also the step that is often forgotten or done quickly because people are time poor, because thinking happens in our heads and conventional approaches don't often provide ways to share that thinking in effective ways. To make thinking collaborative, structured processes are needed to allow people to share their views, hopes and fears about the future. This type of activity doesn't produce immediate quantifiable outcomes of the type we depend on now, and in a data driven, metric obsessed world, taking time to think is often not viewed as useful or productive. Taking the time is critical if we are to move beyond the constraints of today and think in ways that will allow us to both deal with today's challenges **and** be ready to respond when the external environment changes. Strategic thinking puts the future into futures ready strategy.

Strategic Thinking in Practice

Liedtka (1998) makes the point that there is a lot of discussion about strategic thinking as a concept, but less about what it looks like in practice. She suggests we need to understand strategic thinking in as much detail as strategic planning is now understood, and I agree. She identifies five elements that make up strategic thinking:

- **Systems perspective** – the ability to connect the internal organisation with the external environment, to understand the nature of the business ecosystem, making horizontal and vertical linkages across the system from multiple perspectives,
- **Intent-focused** – the focus on the future, the strategic destination that underpins decision making – a view of the future that motivates people in organisations,
- **Intelligent Opportunism** – the ability to leave open the possibility of new strategies emerging (this is critical because the world will continue to change),
- **Thinking in Time** – connecting the past, present and future, using institutional memory and history as a base for thinking about its future, and
- **Hypothesis-driven** – the ability to develop hypotheses and test them in a way that is both creative and critical.

Liedtka (1998, p. 124) sees these five elements as creating a "strategic thinker with a broad field of view that sees the whole and the connections between its pieces … ever open to emerging opportunities". I see strategic thinking as consisting of three main capabilities – the ability to think big, deep and long. tBriefly, here's how I define them.

Thinking Big: do you understand how your organisation connects and intersects with other organisations and the external environment? Do you take a systems perspective?

Thinking Deep: how deeply are you questioning your assumptions? Do you operate from your interpretation of the past, or your anticipation of the future? Will your assumptions today be valid into the future? What might you be missing because you aren't paying attention to your worldview and its assumptions?

Thinking Long: how far into the future are you looking? Do you understand the shape of alternative futures for your organisations? Or, do you expect tomorrow will be more of today?

Thinking Big: Taking a Systems Perspective

What is a system? 'A system is a set of things – people, cells, molecules – interconnected in such a way that they produce their own pattern of behaviour over time" (Meadows & Wright 2008, p.3). Systems are designed to achieve outcomes, and some can survive the impact of changes in the external environment and keep achieving those outcomes. Other systems may not fare so well, and will need to adapt quite radically. Others will fail to adapt and will disappear.

If strategy is developed without taking account of systemic interconnections, without considering how shifts in the external environment might change the organisation and vice versa, then that strategy will be myopic. Leaders in organisations need to learn to see this larger ecosystem of which their organisation is a part, and to focus not on building their piece at the expense of other elements, but to focus on building shared understanding and a common vision (Senge 2003).

The value of systems thinking applies at all levels of an organisation, from individual jobs to departments to the organisation itself and to the industry and beyond. This value emerges as a result of thinking about aligning internal capacity with the reality of a constantly changing external environment and identifying strategy that will ensure organisational viability into the future.

Thinking Deep: Worldview and Mental Models

I've mentioned worldviews (Chapter 3) and cognitive biases were discussed earlier in this chapter but let's recap. Worldviews can be defined as the network of ideas, beliefs, biases, prejudices, social and cultural embedded-ness, and taken-for-granted assumptions through which you interpret and interact with the world, other people and yourself. Worldviews both constrain what you see in the world, and how you interpret the way the world is organised and operates, shape the way in which you see the world and what you notice, and the way the world is organised and operates (Erhard et al. 2010). Because your mind accepts what you are seeing without question, you don't investigate further or challenge your assumptions, leading to superficial interpretations of the implications of change.

Each of us a particular worldview – our way of 'seeing' the world in which we live. We all filter information to make meaning of what we see every day. We use our worldview to create mental models by making judgements about which information is valuable, and which can be dismissed as not relevant. We make these judgements based on assumptions and thinking habits which are deep seated, and often difficult to identify. These assumptions however, have the effect of trapping us in the past, and preventing us from being open to exploring information about changing trends and emerging issues that will affect our futures. Developing depth in the practitioner starts with understanding our worldviews and how they influence our thinking about the future.

When you are designing how to use foresight in your organisation, you will be making decisions about where and when to inject a structured strategic thinking process into your strategy development. One way is to have a thinking workshop before that annual planning extravaganza so that there is time for people to get together and talk, discuss, explore, challenge and just think about the implications of change shaping their organisation's future. I've yet to find an organisation in my world that has been brave enough to hold a thinking workshop, but I've not given up hope!

If thinking workshops aren't yet a possibility, remember that time for strategic thinking conversations needs to be factored into your strategy development processes. These conversations also need to be facilitated or set up in ways that provide a safe space for people to challenge their assumptions and highlight unhelpful assumptions held by others, for the undiscussables to be discussed and for open minds to become the norm.

Thinking Long: Environmental Scanning

Scanning ensures that you take a long-term perspective on change. Instead of looking for changes in your environment today and that's as far as you go, scanning explores how today's change might evolve over the next 10-20 years. It takes your understanding of change from the short term to the long term. Scanning is about ensuring there are no strategic surprises that arrive on your organisation's doorstep. There's a whole chapter on how to scan (Chapter 7) so I'm not going to spend any more time here, expect to say read the chapter and scan often and scan well.

Finally

The aim of strategic thinking is to understand as best we can the long term context of our decisions today, so that we can ensure those decisions are as wise and as robust as possible. To do this, we need to set up systems and processes in our organisations that support strategic thinking and integrate them into strategy development processes.

Most importantly, we as individuals and collectively in our organisations need to be open to recognising that our worldview and our assumptions about the future might be blinkered and that we may not always know what is 'right' or 'best'. We need to recognise that moving beyond the present as the primary focus of strategy will be essential if we are to engage with the future and develop effective and sustainable strategy today that is futures ready.

9   Lessons from the Field

Helping people in organisations use foresight in their strategy development is both rewarding and challenging. As a novice foresighter in 1999, I quickly learned about the power of language to shape how people respond to the 'newness' and 'difference' of foresight, as well as experiencing how people do begin to change the way they think about the future after participating in a foresight exercise. I am still learning with every engagement I do.

This chapter has my lessons from the field, what I've learned as I've worked with people in a wide range of tertiary education institutions, government departments, professional associations and non-profits organisations. As the good people from the now defunct Tomorrow Today wrote about dealing with change and initiating a new order of things: "doing the work is strategic, cultural and political". This applies equally to introducing foresight as well; you will need to address all three areas in your work.

Introducing Foresight

Recognising the need for foresight is unlikely to emerge from routine and embedded strategic planning processes where the status quo is being maintained implicitly. A trigger to force the introduction of foresight in organisations is useful and this is one time when a crisis may be a good thing. When existing ways of making decisions or dealing with change fail, people are often more open to thinking about new ways of doing things.

Without a crisis, the invitation to enter an organisation to use foresight usually comes because one person understands its value and has convinced the organisation to 'give it a go'. This doesn't mean that the organisation is ready for foresight and that there is support for its use. The door is open however, and that is enough to get started.

As indicated in Chapter 5, support from the CEO is a prerequisite when introducing foresight. As a strategic activity, foresight needs to be positioned as something that isn't optional. Being blunt, people are usually too busy with the day-to-day to consider changing what they do unless it is a directive – that's not a criticism, it's a way of coping with the reality of most work in most organisations today. Foresight will be tolerated initially; acceptance will come with time and participation. This sounds like the wrong way to introduce foresight but there are usually many naysayers who will take opportunities to undermine foresight initiatives without this clear directive. Finally, make sure that using foresight is considered work rather than an add-on or optional activity. Without this commitment across the organisation, foresight will drop down the priority list and while people might be willing to use foresight, the urgent will quickly assume more importance than the long term.

Understand Organisational Politics … at least a little

The Vice-Chancellor who brought foresight to Swinburne understood the value of foresight and why Swinburne could benefit from its use. Whenever requested, he provided strong support for foresight activities and workshops. But he wasn't able to provide continuing support on a daily basis and as I outlined in Chapter 2, he did not stop his senior managers from undermining the implementation process. In hindsight, this lack of continuing support meant that foresight at Swinburne was never going to be embedded in that organisation. Organisational politics are part of the landscape and you will need to understand how things get done at your organisation if using foresight to have any chance of succeeding.

Picking the Right People

Goodwill is powerful. With it, most people are willing to give foresight a go, or to treat it in a neutral manner until its outcomes are more obvious. As I learned however, goodwill is always affected by personal agendas and organisational politics. Selecting the right people to 'do' foresight is therefore critical.

Personal goodwill helps, as does the perception of 'political' neutrality and the ability to explain a concept that is different and unknown, and that sometimes sounds a little weird. Bringing in an expert to help with setting up a foresight program might help, but it might backfire too because expertise used in the conventional walk-in, walk-out approach has a limited life and people can feel like they are being told how to think. If you want foresight embedded in your strategy processes, you need it embedded in people's minds and in your organisational DNA. You need people who know the organisation and how to get things done to understand its value. And in that context, goodwill is important to get people to listen, to 'come to the table'.

Start at Both Ends of the Organisation

Plans to introduce foresight into an organisation need to incorporate working with both leaders and staff. Using foresight is collaborative and while someone will have to make a final decision about strategic directions and options, there is no reason that I've yet heard that justifies not including people in the organisation in strategy processes from the very beginning. It takes more work to set up an inclusive strategy process and that's okay. To not include the people who will be implementing strategy in the development of that strategy makes little sense to me, and is a recipe for strategy execution failure.

Inclusive means starting at both ends of the organisation. Convincing senior managers that foresight is valuable is essential in terms of securing support to ensure there are resources and time allocated to it. Demonstrating to people across the organisation how foresight approaches can help them create a longer term context to deal with the busyness of their day to day work and decision making begins to develop a foundation upon which support for foresight can grow at the 'grass roots'. Only then does the possibility of foresight being embedded into the organisation's DNA become possible.

Language

Language, as always, is critical. It matters. When I first started doing foresight work, it took some time for the title of the Foresight Unit to be announced in public without laughter and giggling in the audience. I said nothing in response usually but was astounded that some really smart people, really senior managers thought it was acceptable to direct these jokes in my direction. I tried to not take myself too seriously, but I did. This was important to me and I grew tired of the jokes very quickly. I understand now that to some degree at least, their response was about their lack of understanding of what I was talking about and that's fair enough. The jokes died down but I was wary of using the term foresight without an accompanying clear explanation after that experience.

Foresight also has a language of its own. Use it wisely or you risk turning people off with what they might perceive as jargon that risks making foresight seem like just another management fad. You will need to use your organisation's language and introduce foresight terms carefully. This of course depends on your organisation's foresight readiness. The language you use if you are starting out with foresight will be quite different compared to if you already have processes in place to think about the future in a systematic way.

There were two main messages here. One is that the language of foresight itself is futures focused and not about the concrete business of today. That can be challenging to people who are used to working in the immediate, with the urgent and with data not imaginations. Two is that care must be taken when presenting foresight to ensure you do it in ways that make sense to people in the organisation – you need to start where they are in terms of willingness to move beyond the status quo. Where you are and your foresight knowledge and expertise are irrelevant if you can't bring enough people on the foresight journey with you. Joseph Voros has some words of advice here: 'use skillful means to tailor the (foresight) message to the recipient's ability to receive'. Take care with language – craft your message for your organisation and its foresight readiness.

Contexts Matter

Contexts are important. As with language, an organisation's culture and how it operates will determine to some degree how you implement and use foresight. Building close partnerships with key staff in each area should be a critical part of your foresight implementation process. The influence of contexts also means that presentations about foresight must to tailored to the audience so they are not seen as existing presentations from other organisations used without any consideration of your unique language, structures or process. And ultimately, the future that emerges for your organisation will not be the same as the future that emerges for another organisation. Hines (2003) reminds us of the need to tailor foresight work when he writes that:

what we need is different kinds of futures for different kinds of contexts, and that there isn't one right approach to doing futures work.

Implementation Will Take Time

Implementation will take time – it is a long-term activity and 'brownie points' will not be won quickly. Processes are put in place easily but influencing how people think about the future will take time. Ensure that there is a tangible outcome from everything you do which shows the benefits of this new approach and how it relates to what the organisation is doing today. Open communication, opportunities for involvement, and regularly seeking comment from your community are critical.

Your aim is to embed foresight as a way of thinking and developing strategy to such a degree that a new leader cannot remove it. It becomes the way you do strategy at your organisation. Without this commitment, you will lack the power to take action on the results. As Marcus Barber comments: 'exploring the future in depth and having a good handle on emerging and likely future events is of little value if you are not then willing, able or permitted to take action needed to be better positioned as a result'.

Challenging Status Quo Thinking

One of your biggest challenges will be to help people shift how they think about the future. It's a challenge because there are no future facts. The future is not predictable – it is full of the new and the strange. When confronted with uncertainty and the unknowable, we retreat to explanations based on what is already known. Cognitive biases kick in and all that does is create assumption walls in your thinking – those mental blocks that indicate there is an unquestioned assumption about the future lurking in your brain that needs to be surfaced and tested.

Marcus Barber says that a lesson he learned while at Swinburne was that 'teenagers and senior academics have one thing in common – they're both too smart to be told anything'. He's right. We all have deeply held beliefs that shape how we think about the future. Unless we have an open mind and unless our foresight switch is turned on, we will shut down information that challenges those beliefs, no matter how well researched, presented and delivered that information may be. Unfortunately, not everyone has an open mind.

My view is that one primary success factor for any foresight process is the ability of people to change the way they think about the future, to surface their foresight capacity and expand their worldviews to encompass the past, present **and** future. That thinking shift takes time, is intangible, measurable not by data, sales and other conventional success measures but by how people report their experience of foresight. The point is that no matter how well designed foresight processes are, if people in an organisation don't think about the future in new ways, outcomes will never be as robust and futures ready as they could be. The organisation will be trapped in the status quo with reaction to change the only option.

Challenges You Might Face

Information Overload When You Scan

Scanning becomes easier over time. If you scan regularly, you will become an 'unconsciously competent' scanner. But there will always be a lot of information out there. How do you deal with it so you don't go into information overload? Remember your scanning anchor, while following up leads that look as they might be useful. Trust your insight and intuition about what is credible and what is not is essential – you will soon learn how to identify good sources and what matters. Over time, you will be able to determine fairly quickly what is important and what is not. Filtering tools will help too – as discussed in Chapter 7, there are digital tools now that will help you both do scanning and organise it to save you time.

Time for Scanning

Scanning takes time. To build your skill level, you will need to scan on a regular basis and you need to scan regularly to build up a database. Start with 15-30 minutes every couple of days, and then adjust your time allocation as you get more comfortable with the process. Eventually, you will be scanning all the time, whether you know it or not, so make sure you have a way of easily recording any hits you find for further exploration. The key is to set a schedule for scanning and not change it. If you are managing a scanning process, commit to making the time available for your staff to do their scanning. Ensure they know that scanning is work too, and that you support them spending time on this strategic activity. Encourage them to allocate set times for scanning and to not be distracted by the seemingly urgent work that is sitting on their desk.Stretching your Thinking (or my brain hurts!)

Using foresight will probably require you to retrain your brain to shift the patterns of the past to be more open to the future, and to shift from an operational to a strategic focus. Your brain will start to hurt because you will be in reflexive thinking mode, challenging what you always thought to be acceptable ways of thinking and operating. You will be dealing with complexity and uncertainty. What you think is impossible now just might be plausible in the future, and this asks you to critique how you make sense of your world. That is a truly uncomfortable process, so expect some cognitive dissonance. Remember if your brain doesn't hurt, you are probably not stretching your thinking enough!

The Biggest Challenge to Strategic Thinking: I'm So Busy

One of the first things you will hear when you start talking about strategic thinking is something like: I understand why I need to think strategically, but I'm so busy I can't see how I will make the time to think. When you are asked to think strategically, to reflect on the implications of change for your organisation, you will wonder how you can add it to your already long to do list. Yet, if we take time away from the urgent and commit to strategic thinking processes, the result is a much stronger sense of what is important and will help achieve strategy today and what is actually busy work.

The busyness syndrome (Johnston 2007) has taken over our work lives today. While we complain about how busy we are, how much work we have to do, how many emails we received before lunch, and how stressful it all is, we continue to deny ourselves the time to rethink the paradigm that has generated the busyness and the stress in the first place. While we are all too busy to think, we remain unable to envision and create a more sustainable future for our organisations. We remain trapped in the status quo.

As with scanning, when I work with people to introduce strategic thinking in a formal way to their work, the starting point I recommend is to carve out a minimum of 30 minutes of non-negotiable time on one day a week and keep it sacrosanct. You can explore an issue or challenge you are facing by doing something like the following activities.

- Ask questions such as 'what issues are causing me to wake at 4am in the morning', 'what do I need to know about them?'. Use your scanning and explore those things you need to know more about. Or go to Shaping Tomorrow and see what other people are saying about your issue.

- When you have information available, sit and think about what it might mean, looking for patterns in what you are reading – are people saying the same or different things about your issue? Is there something new or that gives you a new perspective on your issue?

- If you think there is something new, try using a tool like the Futures Wheel (Chapter 6) to explore implications for your organisation.

- Have a conversation with someone who will challenge your thinking about what you are finding and what you think the implications are for your issues.

- If you hit an assumption wall, look for evidence that disproves what you think and supports the change that caused you to utter 'that's rubbish'. While the change may not be relevant now, can you afford not to take it into account now?

Using foresight will always be about balancing a strategic activity with your operational imperatives. Most of us spend the majority of our working time in the operational arena and feel guilty when we move out of that space to focus on other things. Setting time aside for scanning and thinking isn't easy to do in today's work environment, but if you want stronger and more robust strategy, if you want your foresight switch turned on, then both must be priorities in your work schedule and in your organisation's strategy development. Remember that using foresight is about building a long-term context for your decision making today. You want your decisions to be robust over time, not lose validity and usefulness as the world changes. The value of foresight is that is allows you to develop an anticipatory capacity over time – to understand the major factors shaping your organisation's future in ways that will help you make wiser and futures ready decisions today.

10 Parting Words …

Little did I know in 1999 that the Vice-Chancellor's request to me to 'do foresight' would change how I think about the future and my career. In 2008 after 28 years as a university manager, I stopped working in universities to run my foresight practice. My learning journey about foresight has continued since. Both the lack of using foresight in strategy development and its ad hoc use in most Australian organisations has made me more committed to (i) helping people surface their foresight capacity and use foresight to develop futures ready strategy, and (ii) with others, working towards the long term goal of seeing pervasive use of foresight in organisational strategy.

This work takes persistence because it asks people to think in new ways about the future and to let go of deeply held and often sub-conscious beliefs about what will shape the future. It asks them to move beyond their comfort zones. A good foresight process will help people make this thinking shift and seeing the foresight switch go on for people in a workshop is one of the best rewards that comes from doing this work. And once that switch is on, it can't really be turned off. You can't really go back to thinking like you did before surfacing your foresight capacity.

Getting very busy people in organisations to spend the time needed to shift how they think about the future is unfortunately not always possible. You will never convince everyone about the value of foresight and trying to do that would be a waste of your time and energy. Look out for what I call that 'glazed eye syndrome', a clear indicator of a closed mind. If you see that, excuse yourself as soon as possible because chances are you have little hope of getting an engagement or gaining traction in that organisation or with that person. Focus your energy where you can get meaningful outcomes that make a difference. Remember, your energy and time is finite.

Ultimately, human agency is central to foresight work. People create their futures collaboratively not via the input or pontifications of a single senior executive, a keynote speaker or an external consultant. Foresight processes must have people and collaborative processes at their core. Focus your work with the people who either 'get foresight' or who are willing to give you a go in the beginning. I have always said you only need a foot in the door and then it is up to you.

Some Self Reflection Questions

To finish this chapter and the book, I have included two lists below that were developed originally for a client. They offer some questions for you to use to think about the degree to which you are using your own foresight capacity, and the degree to which your organisation has integrated foresight into its strategy processes. The questions are designed as triggers for reflection.

And remember, there are no right answers! You can also take the Foresight Exam on the Shaping Tomorrow site to assess your foresight competence now – their Foresight Guide will help you fill your gaps.

Your Organisation's Foresight Capacity

Does your organisation:

- take a long-term view in its strategy development? If not, what can you do about it?

- explore possible future operating environments to discover new options and identify potential risks?
- have strategy processes that incorporate time for strategic thinking? Do you hold thinking workshops?
- devote sufficient resources to support strategic thinking about possible futures?
- support big picture thinking (taking a forward view), or does it think in silos (status quo)?

Your Foresight Capacity

- Make sure you are busy with the right things?
- Actively seek out alternative perspectives to test the validity of your perspectives on an issue. Do you question your assumptions, no matter how deeply held they are?
- Take the future and future generations into account when you are thinking about strategy?
- Think broadly, deeply and long term about change, and look beyond the mainstream?
- Do you think big picture (take a forward view) or in silos (status quo)?

In the Introduction I wrote: *I also admit I'm asking you to trust me that using foresight in practice is valuable; only you can decide whether I've earned your trust. Read the book before you decide.* Here we are at the end of the book. I hope I have made a strong claim about the strategic value that comes from using foresight that you can accept and that I've earned your trust. Let me know either way if you can and good luck with your foresight journey. Enjoy the challenge, the learning and even the difficulties in being accepted that you will inevitably encounter. And remember to get in touch when you are ready if you have questions or need my help.

References

Ashkenas, R., 2013. Four Tips for Better Strategic Planning. *Harvard Business Review*. Available at: https://hbr.org/2013/10/four-tips-for-better-strategic-planning/ [Accessed February 10, 2016].

Borch, K., Dingli, S.M. & Jorgensen, M.S., 2013. *Participation and Interaction in Foresight: Dialogue, Dissemination and Visions*, Cheltenham: Edward Elgar Publishing. Available at: https://books.google.com/books?id=hNUmvTpD81sC&pgis=1 [Accessed March 3, 2016].

Candy, S., 2015. The Thing from the Future. *Compass Methods Anthology - Association of Professional Futurists*. Available at: http://profuturists.org/resources/Documents/Compass/2015-SE-Compass-MethodsAnthology.pdf.

Choo, C.W., 1999. The Art of Scanning the Environment. *Bulletin of the American Society for Information Science*, 25(3), pp.13–19. Available at: http://choo.fis.utoronto.ca/FIS/ResPub/ASISbulletin/default.html [Accessed March 13, 2016].

Conway, M., 2001. The Swinburne Experience: Integrating Foresight and Strategic Planning. *Scenario and Strategy Planning*, 3(4), pp.12–16.

Conway, M. & Voros, J., 2002. Implementing Organisational Foresight: A Case Study in Learning from the Future. Paper presented at Probing the Future: Developing Organisational Foresight in the Knowledge Economy Conference, Glasgow.

Curry, A. & Hodgson, A., 2008. Seeing in Mulitple Horizons: Connecting Futures to Strategy. *Journal of Futures Studies*, 13(1), pp.1–20.

Davis, G., 2004. Scenarios as a Tool for the 21st Century, Shell International. Available at https://www.pik-potsdam.de/news/public-events/archiv/alter-net/former-ss/2006/programme/31-08.2006/leemans/literature/davis_how_does_shell_do_scenarios.pdf. [Accessed February 24, 2016].

Day, G. & Schoemaker, P.J.H., 2005. Scanning the Periphery. *Harv,ard Business Review*, November.

Erhard, W., Jensen, M.C. & Barbados Group, 2010. *A new paradigm of individual, group and organizational performance*, Available at: http://ssrn.com/abstract=1437027.

Esbjorn-Hargens, S., 2009. An Overview of Integral Theory, *Integral Post*. Available at: https://integrallife.com/integral-post/overview-integral-theory [Accessed February 24, 2016].

Farrington, T., Henson, K. & Crews, C., 2012. The Use of Strategic Foresight Methods for Ideation and Portfolio Management. *Research-Technology Management*, (March-April).

For-Learn, 2006. Delphi Survey. *Online Foresight Guide*, p.6. Available at: http://forlearn.jrc.ec.europa.eu/guide/2_desing/meth_delphi.htm.

Gerstner Jr., L., 1973. Can strategic planning pay off? *McKinsey Insights &Publications*. Available at: http://www.mckinsey.com/insights/strategy/can_strategic_planning_pay_off [Accessed February 10, 2016].

Goddard, J. & Eccles, T., 2013. *Uncommon Sense, Common Nonsense* 2nd. ed., London: Profile Books.

Grim, T., 2009. Foresight Maturity Model (FMM): Achieving Best Practices in the Foreisght Field. *Journal of Futures Studies*, 13(4), pp.69–80.

Hagel III, J., Seeley Brown, J. & Davison, L., 2010. A Brief History of the Power of Pull. *Harvard Business Review*. Available at: https://hbr.org/2010/04/a-brief-history-of-the-power-o.html [Accessed February 10, 2016]

Hamel, G. Moonshots for Managers. *The Wall Street Journal. Available at:* https://blogs.wsj.com/management/2009/02/18/moonshots-for-managers/ [Accessed February 6, 2016).

Heracleous, L. & Jacobs, C.D., 2008. Crafting Strategy: The Role of Embodied Metaphors. *Long Range Planning*, 41, pp.309–325.

Hines, A., 2003. An audit for organizational futurists: ten questions every organizational futurist should be able to answer. *Foresight*, 5(1), pp.20–33.

Hines, A. & Bishop, P.C., 2007. *Thinking about the Future: Guidelines for Strategic Foresight*, Washington D.C.: Social Technologies.

Horton, A., 1999. A simple guide to successful foresight. *Foresight*, 1(1), pp.5–9.

Inayatullah, S., 2004. The Causal Layered Analysis (CLA) Reader. Taipei: Tamkang University Press.

Inayatullah, S., n.d. Using the Future to Explore Visions of Globalization. Available at: http://www.metafuture.org/Articles/UsingtheFuturetoExploreVisionsofGlobalization.htm.

Johnston, S., 2007. *What do you do for a living? A bold new vision for leaders*, Melbourne: Hardie Grant Books.

Keenan, M., 2007. Combining Foresight Methods for Impact. Available at: http://www.mckinsey.com/Insights/Corporate_Social_Responsibility/ Redefining_capitalism?cid=mckq50-eml-alt-mip-mck-oth-1410 [Accessed October 28, 2014].

Liedtka, J., 1998. Strategic Thinking: Can It Be Taught? *Long Range Planning*, 31(1), pp.120–129.

Liedtka, J., 2011. Strategy as Experienced. *Rotman Magazine*, (Winter), pp.29–38.

Lum, R., 2014. *VERGE: A General Practice Framework for Futures Work,* Available at: ttps://visionforesightstrategy.wordpress.com/2014/09/15/verge-a-general-practice-framework-for-futures-work/ (Accessed on February 6, 2016].

Martin, R., 2013. Don't Let Strategy Become Planning. *Harvard Business Review*, 2013. Available at: http://blogs.hbr.org/cs/2013/02/dont_let_strategy_become_plann.html .

Mathews, R. & Wacker, W., 2003. *The Deviant's Advantage: How Fringe Ideas Create Mass Markets*, London: Random House Business Books.

Meadows, D. & Wright, D., 2008. *Thinking in Systems*, White River Junction: Sustainability Institute.

Mintzberg, H., 1994. The Fall and Rise of Strategic Planning. *Harvard Business Review*. Available at: https://hbr.org/1994/01/the-fall-and-rise-of-strategic-planning [Accessed February 6, 2016].

Molitor, G.T.T., 2003. Molitor Forecasting Model: Key Dimensions for Plotting the "Patterns of Change." *Journal of Futures Studies*, 8(1), pp.61–71.

Peter, M.K. & Jarratt, D.G., 2015. The practice of foresight in long-term planning. *Technological Forecasting and Social Change*.

Pfefffer, J. & Sutton, R.I., 2006. *Hard Facts, Dangerous Half-Truths, and Total Nonsense: Profiting from Evidence-Based Management*, Boston: Harvard Business Review Press.

Popper, R., 2013. Foresight Methodology. In L. Georghiou et al., eds. *The Handbook of Technology Foresight*. Cheltenham: Edward Elgar, pp. 44–48. Available at: http://rafaelpopper.wordpress.com/foresight-diamond/.

Raford, N., 2012. From Design Fiction to Experiential Futures. In A. Curry, ed. *The Future of Futures*. Houston: Association of Professional Futurists.

Rohrbeck, R., Battistella, C. & Huizingh, E., 2015. Corporate foresight: An emerging field with a rich tradition. *TechnolEssential Visioning : Overview and Comparative Analysis of Visioning Techniquesogical Forecasting and Social Change.*

Scearce, D. & Fulton, K., 2004. *What if? The Art of Scenario Thinking for Non-Profits*, San Francisco: Monitor Group. Available at: http://www.monitorinstitute.com/downloads/what-we-think/what-if/What_If.pdf. [Accessed October 28, 2014].

Schultz, W.L., 2006. The cultural contradictions of managing change: using horizon scanning in an evidence based policy context. *Foresight*, 8(4), pp.3–12.

Schultz, W.L. 1996. *Essential Visioning : Overview and Comparative Analysis of Visioning Techniques. Available at:* http://www.infinitefutures.com/essays/fs11.shtml. [Accessed October 28, 2014].

Senge, P., 2003. Creating Desired Futures in a Global System. *Reflections: The SOL Journal on Knowledge, Learning and Change*. Ava. ilable at: https://c.ymcdn.com/sites/www.solonline.org/resource/resmgr/Docs/Reflections5-1.pdf.

Sharpe, B., 2013. *Three Horizons: The Patterning of Hope*, Axminister: Triar.

Slaughter, R., 1999. *Futures for the Third Millennium*, Sydney: Prospect Media.

Slaughter, R.A., 2004. *Futures Beyond Dystopia: Creating Social Foresight*, London: Routledge.

Van Der Heijden, K., 2005. *Scenarios: The Art of Strategic Conversation*, Chichester: John Wiley & Sons Ltd.

Voros, J., 2003. A generic foresight process framework. *Foresight*, 5(3), pp.10–21. Available at: http://www.emeraldinsight.com/doi/abs/10.1108/14636680310698379.

Voros, J., 2003. Reframing Environmental Scanning: A Reader on the Art of Scanning the Environment. Melbourne: Australian Foresight Institute, Swinburne University of Technology.

Wilber, K., 2001. *A Theory of Everything: An Integral Vision for Business, Politics, Science and Spirituality*, Boulder: Shambhala.

Wilson, I., 1997. Focusing Our Organizations on the Future: Turning Intelligence into Action. *On the Horizon*, 5(3), pp.3–6. Available at: http://horizon.unc.edu/projects/seminars/futurizing/focusing.html [Accessed February 10, 2016].

Wilson, I., 2006. *From Scenario Thinking to Strategic Action*. Available at: http://horizon.unc.edu/projects/seminars/futurizing/action.asp [Accessed February 6, 2016].

Wooldridge, E., 2010. Rethinking Strategic Planning for uncertain times. , pp.11–12.

About Maree Conway

Maree Conway is a strategic foresight practitioner and researcher based in Melbourne, Australia. She runs Thinking Futures to help people in organisations think about possible futures to inform strategic action and decision making today.

Join Maree in the journey to make the use of foresight pervasive in organisational strategy. Become a Thinking Futures member to have access to foresight resources, services and training. Find out more at: http://thinkingfutures.net

Email: maree.conway@thinkingfutures.net
Web: http://thinkingfutures.net

Made in the USA
Las Vegas, NV
12 November 2020

10731066R00119